What people are saying about …

MIRROR BALL

"In *Mirror Ball*, Matt Redman does just what the title suggests: using his unique experience and gifts to reflect the brilliance of God's love and grace, inviting us into a lifestyle of worship that lights our way and illuminates the world around us. One of the leading voices in worship in this generation, Matt has a fantastic ability to sing with written words and to make the eternal approachable for all. Matt is not only a dear friend, he's a pastor who will lead you well through *Mirror Ball*'s pages."

Louie and Shelley Giglio, founders
of Passion City Church, the Passion
Movement, sixstepsrecords

"Matt has a wonderful way with words. This great book encourages and challenges in equal measure and will be an inspiration to anyone passionate for more of God."

Tim Hughes, worship leader at Holy
Trinity Brompton, London

"Matt Redman is definitely 'a man after God's own heart,' and in *Mirror Ball* he helps us to see the heart, love, passion, and greatness of our God. I could not put this book down until I finished it, and when I did, I was compelled to bow down and worship our glorious Savior. Matt's personal and engaging writing style and profound insights will leave you hungry for more of God and eager to make a difference in your world."

Christine Caine, director of Equip &
Empower and founder of the A21 Campaign

"Matt has been an inspiration to us over the years. Yes, he's written some great songs and led thousands in worship, but it's the kindness of the man that speaks the most. It's his love for God and His people that makes him a mirror ball. Read this book and let the lights come on."

Martin and Anna Smith, authors of
Delirious and *Meet Mrs. Smith*

"Refreshing, challenging, and inspiring all at once, *Mirror Ball* beckons hearts to live as they were meant: shining for the glory of God!"

Phil Wickham, vocalist and songwriter

"Very few songwriters are able to prolifically expand on the ideas that their lyrics convey. Matt Redman is a shining example of one who can. *Mirror Ball* does for readers what his songs have done for worshippers for many years: point people to a great God who wants to shine in them."

Matt Maher, singer and songwriter

"With lyrical phrases and poignant stories, Redman uses his tremendous talent with words to tackle the subject of what it means to live as a worshipper of the triune God. This book is itself a 'mirror ball,' each chapter another angle reflecting the same glorious Light. This is a powerful challenge for all believers to recover our calling as God's image-bearers and to live in a way that displays the radiance of Christ."

Glenn Packiam, executive pastor
of spiritual formation at New Life
Church, Colorado Springs, CO.

MIRROR BALL

MIRROR BALL

LIVING BOLDLY AND
SHINING BRIGHTLY FOR
THE GLORY OF GOD

MATT REDMAN

David C Cook®
transforming lives together

MIRROR BALL
Published by David C Cook
4050 Lee Vance View
Colorado Springs, CO 80918 U.S.A.

David C Cook Distribution Canada
55 Woodslee Avenue, Paris, Ontario, Canada N3L 3E5

David C Cook U.K., Kingsway Communications
Eastbourne, East Sussex BN23 6NT, England

David C Cook and the graphic circle C logo
are registered trademarks of Cook Communications Ministries.

The website addresses recommended throughout this book are offered as a
resource to you. These websites are not intended in any way to be or imply an
endorsement on the part of David C Cook, nor do we vouch for their content.

All song lyrics are used by permission.

All Scripture quotations, unless otherwise noted, are taken from the Holy
Bible, New International Version®. NIV®. Copyright © 1973, 1978, 1984
by Biblica, Inc™. Used by permission of Zondervan. All rights reserved
worldwide. www.zondervan.com. Scripture quotations marked MSG are taken
from *THE MESSAGE*. Copyright © by Eugene H. Peterson 1993, 1994,
1995, 1996, 2000, 2001, 2002. Used by permission of NavPress Publishing
Group. The author has added italics to Scripture quotations for emphasis.

LCCN 2011927113
ISBN 978-0-7814-0578-2
eISBN 978-0-7814-0722-9

The Team: Alex Field, Amy Kiechlin Konyndyk,
Sarah Schultz, Caitlyn York, Karen Athen
Cover Design: Scott Lee Designs, Scott Lee
Cover Image: Shutterstock, #8054332

Printed in the United States of America
First Edition 2011

1 2 3 4 5 6 7 8 9 10

042911

To all my brilliant children: Levi, Jackson, Rocco, Noah, and Maisey. My prayer is that you will each grow up reflecting the love and light of Jesus in this world.

**We are mirrors whose brightness ...
is wholly derived from the sun
that shines upon us.**

—C. S. Lewis

ACKNOWLEDGMENTS

Thanks to:

My radiant wife, Beth. Your fire for God and your passionate life are a privilege to be around. When I think of someone living a big life, I think of you. Thanks for putting up with me writing both a book and an album at the same time. Please remind me to never do that again!

Thanks to my mum, Barbara, for being an incredibly steadfast support to us. Your servant heart has made so many things possible.

Thanks to Lesley for your love and support to us.

Thanks to Tom Redman for so much behind-the-scenes help, and to Lizzie for helping make that possible.

Thanks to our new pastors, Archie and Sam Coates, for welcoming us into the family at St. Peter's with kindness and care.

Thanks to Louie and Shelley Giglio for friendship, direction, and a musical home.

Thanks to Martin and Anna Smith for being wise and faithful friends for so long now.

Thanks to the Grants and the Pytches for inspiring us.

Thanks to Don, Alex, Caitlyn, and all at David C Cook—I am so glad to be partnering with you all. And Alex, a great big thanks for writing such a helpful study guide.

And thank you, Graham Tomlin, for reading through the manuscript and giving some really helpful insights and advice.

Lastly, thanks to so many worship-leading and pastoring friends around the world—your friendships, songs, sermons, and conversations have shaped much of the way I think about worship and therefore much of this book, no doubt. There are too many to list in full, of course, but special thanks to Tim and Rachel Hughes, Jonas Myrin, Chris and Lauren Tomlin, Paul Nelson, Matt Maher, Jason Ingram, Les Moir, Mike Pilavachi, Will and Caroline Kemp, Andrew Philip, Stuart Barbour, Peter Wilson, Christopher Cocksworth, Andy and Michelle Hawthorne, Todd Fields, Ben Cantelon, Ken Costa, Kristian Stanfill, Brett Younker, Nathan and Christy Nockels, Jacob Arnold, Noah Culver, Matt Podesla, Bryan Brown, Tofer Brown, Jon Duke, Robert Marvin, Stephen Bailey, Simon Brading, Nathan and Lou Fellingham, George Mhondera, Graham Kendrick, Andy Piercy, Chris Quilala, Paul Baloche, Don Williams, Bobby Blazier, Jesse and Janet Reeves, Daniel Carson, Travis Nunn, Matt and Laura Gilder, Jim McNeish, Frog and Amy Orr-Ewing, J John and Killy, and Tim and Julie Wanstall.

CONTENTS

FOREWORD

Matt Redman loves American history, which is funny, because he's British. You'd think it would be a bit of a sore spot—but apparently those continental wounds have healed, for Matt is a fountain of random knowledge of all things American.

You might be wondering: How exactly did I come to know this?

Well, Matt brought it up one day while we were cowriting a song about God; specifically, he started talking about the oratory skills and literary content of John Adams. Come to think of it, he's brought up a lot of random facts and figures in our time together—not just about American history, but about life in general. Which gives me a better understanding of why Matt is such a good writer: because his mind is a human storage depot, a sponge of facts and figures. You see, songwriters need the events and happenings of the people and places in the world around them. They become unlikely catalysts of thought of a different sort, reflecting and redirecting both light and insight. As Psalm 139:14 says, "I praise you because I am fearfully and wonderfully made."

When you consider that phrase, you start to see the possibilities of that fear and that wonder being revealed in unlikely places. You begin to see that everything we do reflects back to our Maker as well, be it good or bad. When you understand where the light in our lives comes from, and who it's pointing back at, who we are and what we do become something so much more. *Our lives become mirrors of His glory.* Think of a whole world of mirrors, each follower of Jesus shining and being used by God in a symphony of light heading out in every direction. You can see the whole earth shining for Him. You can see the whole universe and billions of stars in the cosmos. All shining with heaven.

Like a mirror ball.

—Matt Maher, worship leader and songwriter

PREFACE

This book is about living a big, bold, bright life of worship. I hope
as you read these pages you might get a heightened view of Jesus and
grab on to a new confidence of what you can become in Him. May
wonder, love, passion, and justice explode from our hearts and lives,
for the glory of His name.

Matt Redman

1

THE PASSION OF THE CHRISTIAN

It's New Year's Eve in downtown Nashville, and things are getting crazy. There's a mood of fun and festivity everywhere you look. And inside the biggest arena of all, two of the most popular country acts in the nation lead thousands of fans in a celebration of the end of one year and the beginning of the next. The music cranks up loud and the shouts of the audience respond in kind. The truth is, people love to party.

That night in Tennessee, we arrived to prepare for the Passion college gathering. Over the next few evenings the same arena would fill again, and we'd start a party of a different kind. No less volume or excitement—*hopefully more*—but a whole different reason for letting out those shouts of joy. If people can get that excited over December becoming January, what on earth does it look like when over twenty thousand college students get their hearts and heads around the glory and grace of God? What does it sound like when we find ourselves caught up in the epic story of the One who came to this earth, endured the cross, and made a way home for us—all in the name of love and rescue? As loud and as fun as those New Year celebrations might be, shouldn't they become just the faintest whisper when compared with the thunderous shouts and applause that accompany the praise of the King of all heaven? In the words of the old worship hymn, "Hark! How the heavenly anthem drowns all music but its own."

I once met a man who'd survived a shark attack by screaming so loudly that he burst blood vessels in his neck. His ear-piercing cries gave the shark so much of a headache that it gave up the attack and swam away. Where did such a loud scream come from? It came from deep inside him—from the very depths of who he was, crying out for mercy and survival.

So on the last night of the Passion student gathering that year, my good friend Louie Giglio, the founder of Passion, decided we were going to throw the party to end all parties. No low-key affair with some semiloud music and a halfhearted whoop or two—but a full-on, turn-it-up-loud celebration of the Son of God. The point being that if we truly live in the light of Christ and all that He has accomplished, there's a time to be a little bit outrageous in our gathered response to Him.

The day of the worship-fueled party arrived, and things were beginning to happen inside the arena. People hung extra lights and prepared song lists, and everything looked good for some extreme celebration. Apart from one thing, that is. Louie had been excitedly talking about a mirror-ball moment, which he'd planned for a while. At just the right time, during a joyful worship song, he planned to lower this thing, shine some lights on it, and give a little extra visually creative expression to these full-on celebrations. The first time I heard about the mirror ball, it sounded like a good idea—until I entered the arena, that is. Hanging above the center of the stage was a tiny spherical object, and as I strained my eyes to see it, I thought the object certainly looked like a mirror ball. But I was sure this couldn't be Louie's mirror ball: It was tiny—the kind of thing I'd seen every year from the age of seven at my school disco. Yet—I looked around—there didn't seem to be any other mirror balls hanging up there. And so I had to conclude that this must be the one he was talking about. Quite frankly, I was worried. I decided that we were headed for the biggest anticlimax in the history of Christian worship gatherings. Louie had told everyone on the team about this great disco-ball moment that would help lead us in our joyful worship celebrations—when, as far as I could tell, it was going to be a moment of laughter for all the wrong reasons. I wanted to be a good friend and warn him—but he was so pumped about his little mirror ball, I just didn't have the heart.

As it turned out, I needn't have worried. The evening was wonderful. The thousands of students assembling that night to worship Jesus arrived in silence—as we'd been encouraged to do to prepare our hearts for gathered worship. Through songs and sounds and moments of ancient liturgy, we went to the cross. There we recalled the most amazing act of obedience and sacrifice this world has ever seen. We paused for a while, and I was reminded once again that God makes worshippers out of wonderers. As our hearts breathed in afresh the mystery of grace, we exhaled reverent awe and thanksgiving in response. The soul-gripping mystery of Calvary fueled the fires of our praise, and remembrance led us to rejoicing. Next, we began to turn up the volume a notch or two, with heartfelt songs of devotion resounding intensely around the room. In Scripture, Jesus Himself said that out of the overflow of the heart the mouth speaks—and as we stood there in amazement at the grace and glory of God, sounds of joyful thanksgiving tried to find a way out of our hearts.

And then the moment arrived. Mirror ball time. Down from the ceiling came the world's smallest disco ball. I didn't know whether to laugh, cry … or get my binoculars out to actually see the thing.

However, in one bright, shining moment, all of my fears died. Powerful beams of light hit the face of the ball, and suddenly, in every corner of that massive arena, radiance shone all around. Light filled the room. It seemed to glow on every face and shine on every inch of floor, wall, and ceiling. A huge arena filled with light—by way of a tiny little mirror ball. And people partied. In that moment, focusing on the glory of the Savior and celebrating His victories, we shouted for joy and danced with abandon.

It turns out that in all my doubting and questioning of Louie's mirror ball, I'd seriously underestimated the most important factor— the power and brilliance of the beams of light that shone upon it.

In the end, *it was all a matter of light.*

When it comes to a life of worship and mission, the very same rules apply. In and of ourselves we have no light. But in His bright and shining light we are transformed—and begin to radiate the glories of our God to the world around us. You may be feeling totally inadequate, far from ready for that task. But if so, you have forgotten the most important part of the equation. It is not about *you* and your best efforts. It is about the light, power, and love of *Christ* illuminating our fragile lives. As Scripture reminds us, the same God who said, "Let there be light," has made His light to shine in our hearts.

When God shines upon His church, we become a dazzling testimony to His awesome radiance. You may feel ineffective. You might have lost confidence in your ability to shine. You may think you are too small or inconsequential to ever be of any value in the kingdom of God. But no matter at all—for, in the end, it's all a matter of light. *His light.* The life of worship never begins with you. It starts and ends with Jesus.

Back to Nashville for a moment. I left the arena that night inspired by the shouts and the songs that had been poured out in that place. But the mirror ball left a really big impression. It reminded me of our ultimate call as we live on this earth—to shine all around for the glory of God.

Then another thought hit me: So often we equate passion with volume and energy, and surely that can play an important part. But when it comes to true passion, ultimately those things are just the tip of the iceberg—the part most on display. However, God looks beneath the surface, searching our hearts. Yes, God does call us to sing. He calls us to sing loudly, boldly, joyfully, and reverently before Him. Just check out the exhortations in so many of the psalms for evidence. God loves a shout of praise or a joyful noise brought in

His name. These things are great and important ways of expressing the explosive celebrations happening in our hearts. But to complete the integrity of these offerings, God is looking for a people who will take their passion to the next level and begin to shine His light in their everyday lives. A people who will stand in the light of who He is and reflect His wonders for all the world to see. We see the light. We celebrate the light. And we send the light.

Lives Laid Down

Lives of passion step outside the normal and rational and give all they have gladly and generously. I love this definition of passion being made popular by Louie: "Passion is the degree of difficulty we are willing to endure to achieve the goal." Defined in this way, passion becomes a life laid down in extravagant surrender—thoughts, words, and deeds thrown wholeheartedly into the mix even when it costs us something. Or indeed, costs us *everything*.

This definition also brings us right back to the cross. The passion of Jesus shows us the most heightened example we will ever see of "the degree of difficulty we are willing to endure to achieve the goal." At Calvary we encounter the Savior of the world—who, for the joy set before Him, endured the cross and scorned all of its shame. He underwent agonies we could never imagine. If we were to look at the cross simply through the lens of physical torture it would be grueling enough in and of itself. The cross was one of the most gruesome and painful forms of capital punishment this world has ever seen.

Yet this was no ordinary crucifixion. For here was the Son of God—He who was pure and faultless—becoming stained by our sin and shame. The One so accustomed to the peace and joy of heaven encountered the depths of earthly shame, suffering, and pain. He had no sin and instead became sin for us. He who existed in close communion with the Father felt the cruelty and dark loneliness of Gethsemane and Calvary. Add all of these factors together, and you are left with a cross that is not only physically heavy to carry—but one that is unfathomably heavy to bear in spiritual, emotional, and psychological terms. Yet Christ did so. And, astonishingly, He chose to do so. That is the ultimate display of passion.

Be assured, Jesus was not eager to face the agonies of that place. We do not find Him bubbling over with anticipation—completely the opposite. On the eve of His death, the Savior cries out:

> "*Abba*, Father ... everything is possible for you. Take this cup from me. Yet not what I will, but what you will." (Mark 14:36)

A passionate obedience to the Father and an unwavering commitment to His mission see Jesus through the loneliness of Gethsemane and to the cross. This really is the passion of the Christ. And the passion of the worshipper must take on the very same characteristics.

The Scriptures are full of worship songs and devotional music—and in the right place, music can play such a wonderful and unique role in our worship. It's part of how we've been made and a wonderful way to express our devotion to God together. Eugene Peterson writes:

> Song and dance are the result of an excess energy. When we are normal we talk, when we are dying we whisper, but when there is more in us than we contain we sing. When we are healthy we walk, when we are decrepit we shuffle, but when we are beyond ourselves with vitality we dance.[1]

But passionate worship is never a matter of merely getting the words and tune right or raising a loud shout. The true test of our passion for God will always be our lives. If I'm looking for a heightened way to tell God I love Him, the very best way has very little to do with stringing poetic sentences together. It involves a life laid down in service and adoration. The concrete evidence of whether our worship has lived or died in us will always be our lives. We may sing our songs with good intentions, but in the end our lives must become the evidence.

Singing is easy. The proof is always in the living. Or even the dying. Will the music in our hearts subside when the going gets tough? Will we be distracted or discouraged from our cause when the conditions aren't favorable? Will the fireworks of our excited hearts come to nothing more than a momentary spark that fizzles out, never to be seen again? Or could we prove the flames of our passion even in the furnace of difficulty, inconvenience, and endurance?

Passion is not only that which gets us up in the morning—it helps us see it through to the end of the day. Passion finishes what it begins and makes good on its promise of running the race with perseverance and turning good intentions into fulfilled dreams. Passion is always more than a party. It's a story of guts and glory, pain and purpose. And for anyone who has truly encountered the wonder of the cross, it soon becomes a way of life.

2

LOVE WILL GIVE ITS ALL

Some things in life come easily, and there are other things for which we have to labor, toil, and fight. Those things might cost much—but they are worth every ounce of energy, drop of sweat, and tear that is shed. Love is not just a sweet-smelling rose, delicate and fragrant for those who hold on to it. At times it is a battlefield, a place where the stakes are high and devotion expresses itself in hard-won sacrifice.

As I write, it's 3:00 a.m. and I'm sitting in the ICU, looking at my tiny newborn baby son, Levi Samuel Fisher Redman. He is a gorgeous little boy, fearfully and wonderfully made and impossible not to fall in love with. It's been a battle getting him here, and right now we're still in the midst of the fight. At many points in this pregnancy we nearly lost him, and we've prayed to keep this fragile little boy alive. Any pregnancy has its moments of struggle and endurance. But from beginning to end, this one has felt like an intense battle.

Yet here's the strange thing—nothing seems too inconvenient to face or too much to ask of us. For all the toil, stress, and struggle, it is a labor of love. Even in the heaviest moments, our journey has been fueled by delight, not by duty. We have gladly given the most, never the least. We have not rationed our love for Levi as if it were in short supply. Instead we've been delighted to expend every last bit of energy to care for him and make his new little life as great as it can be. Granted, my wife has labored more than I—*literally*. But we have both freely given of our time, energy, and emotion, all in the name of love. As the Scripture says:

> It burns like blazing fire,
>> like a mighty flame.
> Many waters cannot quench love;
>> rivers cannot wash it away. (Song 8:6–7)

True Love

Today's culture sends many mixed messages about what love looks like, more often than not confusing it with lust or infatuation. We see love that leaves, betrays, and walks away for a better offer. We see a distorted love that can't seem to look beyond itself or past its own issues to think about someone else. We see counterfeit love that won't even be there when you wake up in the morning. But if we want to see the whole picture and what love is *really* like, there's no movie, TV show, or pop-psychology book that can help us. *We must come to the cross.* You could search the whole of history in every kingdom and every culture, but you would never find a better example of what love looks like.

> This is how we know what love is: Jesus Christ laid
> down His life for us. (1 John 3:16)

We were hiding from His face, covered by our shame, and lost without a hope. There was nothing we could do to turn our situation around, nothing in our hands to give us a means of escape. But love broke through the darkest night to find us and bring us back home. In the incarnation of Jesus, in His life, His death, and His resurrection we see the mighty God of love in action. It is a love that seeks us, saves us, rescues us, and revives us. It is patient and kind, neither self-seeking nor easily angered. It keeps no record of wrongs. It always hopes, always trusts, and always perseveres. This love breaks down boundaries, presses through uncertainties, and refuses to be stopped by any obstacle in its path. At Calvary itself we witness the purest love this world will ever see. It is an act so mysterious and magnificent that we shall be singing about it through all eternity. The cross of Jesus has many layers—in its complexity we find such themes as justice, sacrifice, and suffering; obedience, endurance, and hope. But right there in the center, making sense of them all, we find love.

The love of Christ goes far beyond feelings and much deeper than words. Feelings will often play a part in love, but they are never the whole picture.

We were not saved by God's feelings. We were rescued by the sacrificial, blood-soaked struggle of God's love in action. Yes, the love of Jesus plays out in vulnerability, humility, and obedience at the cross. But it is not a passive love. At Calvary, Jesus runs headlong into the fray, engaging intensely with all that stands in His path. Words like *grace* and *mercy* can sound so warm and carefree in certain contexts—but there is nothing soft or fluffy about them in this place. There is blood on the battlefield and a tremendously painful cost in His act of submission. The love of Jesus is not just tender affection or heartwarming kindness. It is not always the softened, blurry-edged picture we might see on our Christmas cards. This is a bold and brave love, journeying into the thick of the fight to rescue the objects of its affection. In those moments of deep surrender at the cross, Jesus fights the good fight, determinedly devoted to His Father and loving all of mankind with every labored breath.

God is love—and through the life of Jesus we see that love in nonstop action. Sometimes it is still and peaceful like a gently flowing stream. At other times it overturns temple tables in a rage, standing up for justice and reverence. We must have the whole picture—the incarnate, active, passionate, surrendering, dying, rising, ascending, reigning Jesus who moves in love and rules in power.

As well as demonstrating the essence of love at Calvary, Jesus gave many other teachings on the subject during His days walking the earth. He told us we can't love both God and money. He reminded us that those who obey His commandments are the ones who really love Him. These are not polite, sterile descriptions of a mild, soft-textured love. They speak of an all-consuming and gutsy offering made in reply to the God who loved us first.

Jesus also taught us that those who have been forgiven much will love much (Luke 7:47). Worship is a reflex of the ransomed heart, never an empty religious ritual or a hollow act of self-deprivation. It is love flowing freely and absolutely from heart, mind, and soul in response to all we have received.

Real love cannot be scheduled or rationed, and it never comes with conditions attached. If our habit is to love God only in the convenience of a Sunday church service and then congratulate ourselves for our supposed devotion, we're in for a shock. For that may not be love at all. The same applies to the person who will give to God only when life is easy and everything is working out favorably. If we say we love God yet stay away from the altar when the journey gets tough, confusing, or complicated, our devotion is very shallow. We can put no conditions on our offerings to God, for He makes no deals and accepts no bribes. Real love makes no disclaimers in the fine print. It has no escape clauses or money-back guarantees. It is faithful, vulnerable, and all consuming—flowing willingly and totally from our hearts, our lips, and our lives. Declarations of love without the accompaniment of obedience are an uncashable check. There appears to be a signature, and at first glance the words and figures all seem to agree, but in reality, the funds are lacking and the account is empty. These empty declarations are worth nothing more than the paper they are written on. And this is also true of the songs we sing if the bank balances of our lives have been spent elsewhere and there is nothing left to give to God.

Love gives of itself whether it's convenient or inconvenient. It operates on joyful heights—but also in the valley of the shadow. It overcomes pain and overturns obstacles. It keeps its promises even when it hurts. Love gives imaginatively and outrageously. It surrenders itself generously, never begrudgingly. When there is much at stake, love will give its all.

Love and Faithfulness

After the events of the cross and resurrection, Jesus meets with Peter, and the lessons in love continue. Following the disciple's failure to acknowledge Jesus on the day of His death, the risen Savior has a question for him: "Do you truly love me?" (John 21:15).

He goes on to ask this same question two more times. And then after each time Peter answers, "You know that I love you," Jesus urges him, "Feed my sheep" (vv. 15–17). There are many themes and ideas implied in His words here, but one of them surely is a call to action. For we can tell Christ we love Him again and again and again—we can whisper it, shout it, or sing it. But in the end, only a life of devotion will breathe meaning into these words. Jesus tells Peter how he can put his spoken declaration of love into action— "Feed my sheep." And from that moment on we witness Peter doing just that—faithfully ministering to the people of God as his act of worship. He completes the integrity of his spoken responses with an obedient and consistent life.

In Psalm 85:10 we read a beautiful phrase: "Love and faithfulness meet together." That is to say, they hang out together. They frequent the same places and enjoy each other's company. Where you find love, right there alongside it you will encounter faithfulness. Love does not cheat, nor does it quickly leave when the going gets tough. For better or for worse, for richer or for poorer, in sickness and in health, love will always remain faithful.

If you were to simply observe the media, you'd think that true faithfulness was an antiquated tradition that died out long ago. TV drama story lines ooze adultery and unfaithfulness. Movie screenplays are structured around tales of disloyalty and treachery. Day after day, newspaper headlines speak of scandal and affairs. In our society, integrity seems as though it's hanging on the gallows, done away with for our amusement and entertainment.

But in the kingdom of Jesus, faithfulness is alive and well. It is not like a genetic code that is present in one generation but missing in the next. The psalmist reminds us: "His faithfulness continues through all generations" (Ps. 100:5).

The steadfastness of God never misses a generation, and His constant heart never skips a beat. He is utterly consistent in all of His ways. And we, so prone to inconsistency and instability, must look to Him as the remedy for all our ills and the solution to every dilemma. The more we fix our eyes upon Jesus, the more we feed upon His Word, the more we know the Holy Spirit's power and presence at work in our lives—the more we will become like Him. Outwardly we may waste away and deteriorate over time. But inwardly, the world is entirely different. Those who live in the knowledge, nearness, and love of Jesus will be transformed.

You may not be where you're aiming to be, but I can bet you're not where you once were. Look back over a couple of weeks or months, and you may indeed see the same old inconsistencies raising their ugly heads in your life. Perhaps there are still patterns of speaking or thinking, or habits and addictions that don't seem compatible with a life of reverent worship. But take a look a little further back—survey your life from when you were first adopted into His love. See how, over the years, you've taken giant leaps forward in faith and made holy progress in your walk with Him? Yes, the power of Jesus could change you in an instant—*and at times it will*. But in other seasons He transforms us moment by moment, little by little. Sometimes we hardly seem to notice it—until we look back over our journey and realize that we look more like Jesus now than we ever did before.

Those inconsistencies in us will have to die at some point— for God is light and in Him there is no darkness at all. He has a great hunger to see holiness at work in our lives. But along the way His patience and power continue to work on us in tandem—His charitable grace and stunning glory kindly but sternly renovating our lives each day. The life of a worshipper is never at a standstill.

God reveals, and we reply. God acts, and we are amazed. God shines, and we reflect. This is the life of worship. This is the beautiful rhythm of revelation and response that occurs when our hearts, minds, and souls encounter the wonders of God. Yet in all the shining, seeing, and reflecting that goes on, another astounding dynamic begins to occur: *We become more like Him.* Charles Spurgeon expressed it so powerfully: "Nothing beautifies a person like praising God. To plunge our whole nature in adoration adorns the spirit."[1]

In worship, beholding is becoming. The more of Jesus we see, the more like Him we shall become. To see Jesus, *really see Jesus,* is to be changed.

3

BIG GOD, BIG LIFE

Everyone who's ever lived a big, risky life for God started off with a good dose of revelation. You can be sure that grace and glory were not tiny, unimportant blips on their spiritual radars; rather, these were major themes infusing every part of their lives. When the majesty and mercy of God really take hold inside us, worship explodes out in every possible direction. A life of daring and devotion is never the result of halfhearted duty, though empty religious rituals might manage on such an appetite. But real worship cannot exist on a diet of apathetic intrigue or indifferent nods to the truth of God. If we are frustrated by a life that seems too boring or ordinary, a great big view of God is just what we need. The best and most enduring praise always flows from an amazed and thankful heart.

Many things may impress us or inspire us in this life, such as sporting endeavors, scientific achievements, or artistic merit. And every now and again we witness an achievement way outside the realm of normal human expectation, and we are led to the edge of wonder. The day a man first set foot on the moon was such an event.

Off the Charts

In a masterful speech on May 25, 1961, President John F. Kennedy set his sights on space exploration and declared, "Now it is time to take longer strides."[1] In particular, the aim was to put a man on the moon by the end of the decade. It was a brave leadership moment—a goal that at the time seemed so far out of reach. And yet in July 1969—just before the end of the decade—that goal was achieved. With an estimated 450 million people watching around the world, a man set foot on the moon.

I recently had the privilege of visiting NASA in Houston with astronaut Michael T. Good, to whom I am hugely grateful. My personal highlight was seeing the original mission control room. It was quite a thrill to sit there in the flight director's chair and look around the room, thinking back to those July 1969, Apollo 11 moments. Marveling at what was achieved, I was also struck by just how antiquated some of that 1960s technology appeared now. The people at NASA told us that there is more processing power in the iPhone than there was in all those mission control computers combined. And yet remarkably, using this equipment, NASA put a man on the moon.

It's no wonder that at the time, some people thought the moon mission was some kind of elaborate hoax—it just seemed so far beyond our normal capabilities. With great vision, bold leadership, and the team efforts of a nation, those moments took the hearts and minds of people all over the world to the edge of wonder. On that day in the summer of 1969, those "longer strides" JFK dreamed of became Neil Armstrong's "one small step for [a] man, one giant leap for mankind."

Yes, at times human endeavor may take us to the edge of wonder. But the worship of Jesus is in a category of its own. The splendor and story of our God can propel us into a realm of awe and astonishment like no one and nothing else. A man walking on the moon is one thing. The God of all time and eternity treading the earth in human flesh is something on a whole different level. When the worshipper tries to measure the ways and wonders of God, those ways and wonders are found to be quite simply "off the charts." Anyone who truly encounters Jesus comes away awed and wowed and loved into a big life of worship.

If we are spiritually shallow or bored, we will be unreliable and unadventurous in our lives of devotion to Christ. Small doses of revelation lead to tiny lives for God. Anyone who ever lived a big life for Jesus journeyed with a great big view of who He is. The Christian walk is not survival of the fittest or simply a case of guts and grit. The life of the Christian worshipper will of course involve determination and constant decisions to endure to the end, but ultimately, you should not have to create some kind of credible testimony to His name. *Worship doesn't start with you.* It begins and ends with a merciful, majestic, and powerful God. The revelation of our God keeps us in the fight even when times get tough, and the wonder of Him fuels our every step. We are wide-eyed worshippers, stunned by glory and strengthened by grace.

God shines in His eternal brilliance, and somewhere deep inside us the lights go on. Over the years, I have had the privilege of sitting at the feet of some great leaders. I have borrowed and devoured many gems of leadership wisdom and advice on what it means to live effectively for Christ. I've sat through messages in conferences all over the world and have heard some of the most powerful communicators teach on how to live and lead effectively for Jesus. I value this greatly and will never take it for granted that I get to spend time in these kinds of environments. But I also know that for all the good these teachings provide, they will never be a substitute for what occurs when a person beholds the glory of God. Getting educated is a good thing—indeed, a great thing. But when it comes to living a powerful spiritual life in the kingdom of God, education will never outweigh encounter, and information will never beat revelation. In the best-case scenario, these things walk hand in hand—each informing the other. At the end of the day in our spiritual walk with Christ, "what you know" must always remain the servant of "who you know."

It is possible to watch Christianity from a certain distance and never really experience its transforming power. You may simply be an onlooker who studies Christ from afar and never really experiences an enriched and empowered life. But when we get closer to the action, everything changes. When we begin to live in close proximity to Christ, we become caught up in the power, wonder, and splendor of who He is. And from that moment forward, change is on the way. We begin to make waves in our social circles, turning ordinary conversations toward the extraordinary. We may inject mercy and kindness into situations where they are much needed but very rare. We begin to participate in the kingdom of God at work in a way that gives everyday events eternal significance. In our hearts we start to believe as possible things that other people cannot even begin to imagine. And before long we are taking a leap of faith that everyone else around us thinks is too great a stride. And this is exactly the kind of transformation that God delights to see in us.

As the great cricketer and missionary C. T. Studd reminds: "Christ does not want nibblers of the possible, but grabbers of the impossible."

At this point, please don't rule yourself out.

You may be thinking that these kinds of activities don't suit your personality type or match up with your track record so far in life. But it is not a case of whether you are an introvert or an extrovert, an experienced or novice Christian. This is not about your personal history or how dynamic you may or may not have been up until now. It is not about the situations you found yourself in during the past or even your present circumstances. You may be rich or poor, young or old. You may be sitting for your first exams or holding a seat of power and prominence in business or government. You may be a singer or a janitor. You may have a voice in the corridors of power or simply some influence at your family dinner table. You may run a high-powered organization or drive to school each day with the children in whom God has entrusted you to invest your life. Wherever you are and whoever you are, Jesus has not written you off. And therefore, by default, you must rule yourself in.

If you are still having trouble believing this, then simply look at the disciples in the early church. This was not a group of obvious world changers by any shape or means. The disciples were ordinary people with something extraordinary happening inside them. The eyes of their hearts had been opened to the glory and grace of the Son of God. The same Spirit that raised Christ from the dead was now alive and at work inside them, and from that moment on it was impossible for things to stay the same. They looked upon Jesus and started to believe the truth of who they could become in Him. As a result, they saw more clearly and dreamed more extravagantly. They obeyed more readily and trusted more deeply. And here's the most beautiful thing of all: *All of this could be true for any one of us.* The formula remains the same today. God's strength is far greater than our weakness, and God's radiance is able to overpower any dullness inside us.

Big Lives

I love the story of George Whitefield, a radiant and radical worshipper from the eighteenth century. This renowned preacher man came from a poor background and became the best-known speaker of his time, delivering over eighteen thousand sermons. George's father passed away when George was just two years old, and growing up, George often skipped school, leaving education at age fifteen to work at the pub where he'd been born. Measles in childhood gave him eye problems for the rest of his life, and in fact he was never a very healthy man. No one would have looked at George Whitefield early on and described him as an extraordinary man screaming with potential. Quite the opposite in fact—Whitefield's life seemed full of struggle and limitation.

But by the time he got into his early twenties this bold and brave man was preaching to crowds of tens of thousands. He traveled far and wide in his life, spending an estimated 780 travel days at sea on his many transatlantic crossings. He persevered through many a stormy horseback journey in order to take hold of all to which God had called him. Those who heard him called this man the "prince of preachers" because he helped change the spiritual climate of England and North America.

The key in all of this, of course, was a great big view of Jesus. In Whitefield's own words:

> I would be so overpowered with a sense of God's Infinite Majesty that I would be compelled to throw myself on the ground and offer my soul as a blank in His hands, to write on it what He pleased.[2]

Others also recognized what was behind the fantastic fervor and endurance seen in Whitefield's life and ministry:

> If it be enquired what was the foundation of his integrity, or of his sincerity, courage, patience, and every other valuable and amiable quality, it is easy to give the answer. It was not the

excellence of his natural temper, nor the strength
of his understanding; it was not the force of his
education—no, nor the advice of his friends. It
was no other than faith in a bleeding Lord—faith
of the operation of God. It was a lively hope of
an inheritance incorruptible, undefiled, and that
fadeth not away. It was the love of God shed
abroad in his heart by the Holy Ghost.... From
this source arose that torrent of eloquence which
frequently bore down all before it; from this
that astonishing force of persuasion which the
most hardened sinners could not resist. This it is
which often made his head as waters and his eyes
a fountain of tears.[3]

In other words, though he had developed many admirable
qualities, it was not ultimately his personality, wisdom, peer group,
or education that effected so much change in and through the life of
George Whitefield. The strength and effectiveness of his efforts were
the reflex action of a man consumed and amazed by the radiance of
His God. The magnificent revelation of Jesus Christ changes a person.

When Whitefield died on September 30, 1770, the hymn writer
John Newton described his life as "a burning and shining light ...
raised up to shine in a dark place."[4]

And biographer John Richards Andrews summed up it like this:

It may be said with truth that few men ever lived
so near to God, enjoyed so much of the Divine

presence in the soul, or so constantly sought to glorify the Redeemer, as did George Whitefield.[5]

A man like Whitefield is a spiritual hero to many, and it can be a great thing to have spiritual heroes. There are many throughout the Bible and in history who have set good examples for us believers to follow.

Another personal hero of mine is the hymn writer Charles Wesley. With his brother John he helped build a movement of worshippers around England, a movement that shaped the nation. And along the way he managed to write around 6,500 hymns. He wrote hymns and poems on every imaginable theme and topic, digging deep into the nature, attributes, and story of God—songs about helping people see God and sing to Him. Equipped with not much more than a horse, a few chords, and the truth, just like his contemporary Whitefield, this seemingly ordinary man contributed to the spiritual temperature of a spiritually needy country.

The only real danger in having these kinds of heroes is that sometimes the heights of what they achieved set a benchmark we think we will never attain. This is not a helpful mind-set, nor is it a perspective based on truth. We must always be reminded that these were not human beings with mental or physical capacities beyond belief. For the most part these people did not even stand out from the crowd as ideal candidates to achieve great things. Time and time again we take a close look at the lives of those we look up to in this way, and we find them to be normal people caught up in the power and wonder of an amazing God. They are heroes of the faith, yes. But they are not superheroes.

On my bad days I might read about someone like Charles Wesley and allow his achievements to become a stumbling block in my own journey. I could end up depressed that in twenty years I've written fewer than two hundred worship songs, but somehow in his life of ministry he was on the way to seven thousand compositions! It'll never be my aim or claim to be even in the same league in terms of song output. But regardless, I must keep my eyes on my own race and hold on to this simple truth—that Wesley and I draw from the same spring of inspiration and are strengthened by the same source of power. It is indeed "Christ in *Wesley* the hope of glory," yes. But it is equally "Christ in *me*"—I hold on to the very same glorious hope. Whether your spiritual mentors or heroes are from a former age or are still living today, the same is true for you. Great men and women of God in the past were as dependent on the power of God to strengthen them in their weakness as we are here today.

This is true of our biblical heroes too. God's strength at work in their frailty gives us much hope for our own walks of faith. Most often they were not the top of the class, nor were they groomed to function at a level higher than everyone else in society. A long line of biblical heroes points us to the likes of Moses (a reluctant public speaker), Gideon (a man with a fear-filled heart), David (an unlikely warrior), and Peter (a guy who was all bark and no backbone). But each and every one of these worshippers was wowed by the glory of God and went on to accomplish astounding things in His power. By including their ordinary beginnings in these biblical accounts, God reminds us that we can also play a part in His story and be used by Him more than we ever dreamed or imagined possible. Studying the power of God at work in these ordinary lives brings a new and heightened confidence to our own hearts. "Anything is possible" ceases to be just a casually used phrase and instead becomes a deep spiritual truth at work in our everyday lives.

We see this confidence time and time again in the book of Psalms. On some occasions the psalmist talks to himself, reminding his heart and mind of the reality he is living in:

> Though an army besiege me,
>   my heart will not fear;
> though war break out against me,
>   even then will I be confident....
> I am still confident of this:
>   I will see the goodness of the LORD
>   in the land of the living. (Ps. 27:3, 13)

His confidence in God becomes optimism for life. It is the positive, bright-thinking of a man who rests securely in the strength and surety of his God:

> With Your help *I can* advance against a troop;
>   with my God *I can* scale a wall....
> He makes my feet like the feet of a deer;
>   he enables me to stand on the heights. (Ps. 18:29, 33)

Such confidence is not based on arrogance. Instead it flows from a steadfast faith in God, and as such, it is a beautiful thing. Just like the psalmist back then, we could do with developing a few "*I can*" affirmations for our own lives today:

> "With my God *I can* make a difference in my workplace."

> "With my God *I can* stand firm at school when all around me are living a different way."

> "With my God *I can* overcome this addiction."

> "With my God *I can* dwell in joy, even living in a tough environment."

Add your own affirmation to this list, for these are not empty self-help mantras. They are biblical, truth-filled declarations that flow from the lips of a child of God. Just like the psalmists who journeyed before us, we, too, believe that in our God we can stand "on the heights."

Four Minutes

For many years the four-minute mile seemed like a bridge too far for the human body. Many doctors and scientists said it was physically impossible for someone to run a mile in under four minutes. From the years 1931 to 1945 the record for the fastest mile was broken on ten different occasions. But then for the next nine years the record remained unbeaten, standing at a time of 4 minutes, 1.3 seconds. The prevalent thinking was that nobody could break through this time barrier and run a mile in under four minutes.

And then on the sixth of May in 1954 a twenty-five-year-old medical student named Roger Bannister completely obliterated the prevalent thinking. Competing in Oxford, England, he crossed the finish line in a time of 3 minutes, 59.4 seconds. But here's the fascinating thing—*it didn't take long for others to do the same.* Within forty-six days an Australian athlete named John Landy had also broken the four-minute barrier, taking an astonishing one and a half seconds off Bannister's already groundbreaking time. It seems the four-minute challenge was just as much a mental barrier as it was a physical one. To date, well over a thousand people have recorded under-four-minute mile runs.

In much the same way, our spiritual heroes from the Bible and from church history may become our "Roger Bannisters." They help banish the idea of the impossible and encourage us that in spiritual terms we can also become "four-minute milers."

We must take on the same mind-set as Caleb in the Old Testament. In Numbers 13, we find him brimming with faith and optimism while his peers are completely paralyzed by negativity and doubt. Sent on ahead to explore the land of Canaan, which God promised them, all twelve men came back assured of the goodness and richness of the land they had seen. But fear of the large fortified cities and their current inhabitants made most of these men shrink back from the promise of providence that stood before them. Only Caleb brought a faith-filled perspective and silenced them all, declaring:

> "We should go up and take possession of the land,
> for we can certainly do it." (Num. 13:30)

Despite Caleb's confident report, fear spread throughout the camp, and the people's hearts melted with fear (Josh. 14:8). As a result not one of the doubters ever got to reach that land flowing with milk and honey. Caleb, however, kept walking in the promise:

> "But because my servant Caleb has a different spirit
> and follows me wholeheartedly, I will bring him into
> the land he went to, and his descendants will inherit
> it." (Num. 14:24)

Many more obstacles and battles ensued along the way, but finally Caleb, eighty-five yet as strong and vigorous as ever, received the fullness of the promise. He came to enjoy the land he'd looked upon with eyes of faith all those years before. We can take so many lessons from this story and let them adapt our outlook regarding the promises and purposes standing before us. Caleb's faith was not a blind faith—he operated in obedience to the voice of God, seeing all the same obstacles that his fellow explorers had witnessed but clinging to the words God had spoken: "The land ... *which I am giving* to the Israelites" (Num. 13:2).

Caleb took into account the various barriers to achieving the goal, but those barriers did not rock his confidence in God. He knew that the promises of God far outweighed the plans of men. Sometimes we ourselves cannot see a way through an obstacle to the fulfillment of our vision—but if God has spoken, we need never shrink back. We worship the God who makes a way where there seems to be no way. Caleb's confidence in this promise brought much glory to God and much favor into his own life.

But note how the fullness of the promise did not unfold immediately. There were many years of endurance and obedience and no doubt many times of consistently choosing to walk the path of faith and hope. The same will be true for our own lives. God has many purposes to unwrap and many places of hope for us to take heart. But the promise may not always find fulfillment quickly or easily. At times in our lives we may face stress, struggle, and lack of patience in God's promises for us. These factors do not mean God has exited the building. We must hold on to hope, never reduce the dream He placed within us, and let the promises of God echo around our hearts and minds as we wait for the fullness of all that has been ordained.

The story of Caleb tells us this: *God does not like being underestimated.*

When we stay within our comfort zone and fail to trust Him for the big things, it's *dishonoring* to God and *disadvantageous* to us. But when we trust God against the world's odds and act upon the promises of God, He will gain much glory, and we will not be left unsatisfied.

The Possible and the Impossible

We see something of this trust dynamic at work in the angel Gabriel's appearances to both Zechariah and Mary in the opening of Luke's gospel. This fearsome angelic being appears to Zechariah and announces that he and his wife, Elizabeth, will soon conceive a child and that their son (John the Baptist) will go on to play an important part in the story of God. Yet Zechariah's faith is too small to handle this thought, and so he questions the validity of the angel's announcement:

> "How can I be sure of this? I am an old man and my wife is well along in years." (Luke 1:18)

He can't get past his current circumstances and move into the realm of faith and trust. It may not even be just the present that is holding him back from believing God's promise. Perhaps disappointment from the past weighs heavily on his shoulders—so much so, he cannot entertain the thought that God can make a way after all these years. At times we are tempted to do the same, knowing deep down that God has spoken but not daring to believe the dream for lack of faith or fear of disappointment.

Contrast this with the angel Gabriel's similar announcement to Mary later in the same chapter. Upon hearing the astounding news of what will soon happen in her life, she, too, asks a question. But the nature of her inquiry does not concern the validity of what the angel Gabriel just announced—instead it's a practical query based on the assumption that what she has just heard will indeed come to pass. In her response, then, Mary affirms in faith that she believes this absolutely extraordinary prediction will indeed come true:

> "I am the Lord's servant.... May it be to me as you have said." (Luke 1:38)

These two contrasting stories give us lessons in the *possible* and the *impossible*. Zechariah highlights that without faith it is *impossible* to please God (Heb. 11:6). The angel Gabriel rebukes Zechariah's lack of belief; it's clear that such a response is offensive to the heart of God when He has spoken in such a clear way. But the opposite is true in Mary's story; her response affirms her belief in the angel's words—that "nothing is impossible with God" (Luke 1:37).

If we live our lives with low expectations in God, we will rob ourselves of a fulfilled life and massively dilute the honor that is due Him. If instead we can step into the realm of faith, we will bring pleasure to the heart of God and enjoy the wonder of adventuring in His purposes. When God has spoken to us, we can be sure of what we hope for and certain of what we do not yet see.

It's never too late to live a big life. If you have ruled yourself out, then rule yourself back in. God can take the lowliest of circumstances, the humblest of beginnings, the most rebellious of life histories, or the shiest of personalities and make something amazing happen for His kingdom. You might travel to distant lands, making a mark everywhere you go for the name of Christ. Or you may never rack up a single air mile and instead live large, influencing your circle of family, friends, and neighbors. You might be an investment banker or a baker, a comedian or an astronaut. You could be a classroom assistant or a cosmonaut. But if you live with a grand view of your high and holy God, you have the potential to make a lasting impact for the glory of His name.

Just as the laws of physics have not changed since the times of our biblical and historical heroes, so, too, the spiritual dynamics in the kingdom of God remain unaltered. The God of Moses, Gideon, Whitefield, and Wesley is our God today. The simple equation goes something like this:

> **God's power**
>
> **+**
>
> **my weakness**
>
> **=**
>
> **anything is possible.**

You do the math.

4

DROPS IN THE OCEAN

I want to return to my NASA visit for a moment. It was not simply the height of the achievement that impressed me that day—but also the manner by which it was achieved.

Yes, I was struck by the optimistic thinking of JFK and his government. But I was also compelled by how people got behind the vision, rose up as one, and worked together to achieve the goal. This was a tremendous national adventure involving a huge collective enterprise and massive public finances. The president did not fulfill this dream alone—he was clear in his visionary speech that for this to become a reality the nation would have to go to the moon *together*.

And that is exactly what happened. All in all, over four hundred thousand engineers, scientists, and technicians worked on Apollo 11[1]—and around seventeen thousand people were involved directly or indirectly in the take-off procedures on launch day.[2] Not to mention the financial contribution made by American taxpayers. This was a gigantic team effort.

This page from the history books can inspire us today. The truth is this: All the big dreams and visions we work toward are within reach if we will harness our gifts and energies and pull together in one direction. So many goals that might never be achieved by an individual can be brought into being by working in community. We underestimate just how much power and potential we have when we work and move as one body. In his book *Courageous Leadership,* Bill Hybels asks us to consider who we are as the church and what we could be capable of in this world:

> Still to this day, the potential of the local church is almost more than I can grasp. No other organization on earth is like the church. Nothing even comes close.[3]

Together We Are the Church

We've seen encouraging evidence of this in the last few years through the Passion college movement. These students prove the point that *together we are so much better.* When you have twenty-two thousand students gathered in one place at one time, you can make serious strides for the kingdom of God. So each year Louie Giglio has announced "Do Something Now," a series of objectives that, if achieved, would touch lives all around the globe. Among the challenges were providing wells for villages in India, funding surgeries for children, and rescuing women from sex slavery in the Philippines.

In 2011 Louie presented these goals and told everyone gathered that meeting all of these targets would require us to raise a total of half a million dollars in our few days together. Now bear in mind that these are *college students*. We're not talking about people with salaries that have increased nicely over the span of their careers. Nor are we dealing with folks who've had decades to put aside a certain level of savings and build up some kind of portfolio. No, these are just ordinary college students. Let's be honest: Not everyone would bet on their reaching these lofty objectives.

The four days of the Passion conference passed quickly, and throughout that time you could feel a sense of faith building—a sense that perhaps we really could meet those gigantic needs. And perhaps if we all came together as one, as the church, we really could change lives all over the planet.

On the last morning of the 2011 event, anticipation was building. Would Louie come to the stage with bad news and tell us we'd done well, but not well enough? Would he apologize and admit that $500,000 dollars is really just a step too far and say that it had been unfair to ask this of college students? Not likely. In fact these twenty-two thousand students gave way above what was asked for and weighed in with gifts of more than $1.1 million in their giving. It was a phenomenal moment. We could have come together, sung our songs, and returned home happy. But now we went with an even greater spring in our step—humbly and happily knowing that God had taken the little we could all afford to give and had transformed it into a sizeable gift that would affect lives and communities in many different nations.

Here are some of the inspiring totals from that day:

- Clean Water Goal—Raise $75,000 for 15 wells in villages in India. Given: 24 wells!
- Micro-finance Goal—Provide 200 small business loans for Afghan entrepreneurs totaling $40,000. Given: 387 loans!
- Bibles Goal—Give away 20,000 New Testaments to unreached in Colombia at $20,000. Given: 31,554 New Testaments!
- Feeding Children Goal—Feed 1,000 at-risk children in South Africa for one year at $50,000. Given: Feeding 2,225 children!
- Homes Goal—Build 15 homes in Haiti at a cost of $54,000. Given: 39 homes!
- Sponsor Children Goal—Sponsor 150 children and provide family essentials at a cost of $100,000. Given: 442 children sponsored!
- Human Trafficking Goal—Create restoration and a future for 10 girls trapped in sex slavery in Bolivia at a cost of $36,000. Given: 22 girls rescued and restored!
- Surgeries for Children Goal—Raise $50,000 to fund 50 hydrocephalus surgeries in Uganda. Given: 141 surgeries!

- Rescue Women Goal—Provide $45,000 to fund 10 rescue operations to free sex slaves in the Philippines (each operation frees 15 women on average). Given: 29 rescue operations!
- Plus: Create a college fund for Haitian earthquake survivor Therissa Leo. Given: $23,106!

As well as reaching all of these fantastic amounts, the students brought with them 18,400 new towels and 88,000 pairs of socks for the homeless in shelters throughout the city of Atlanta.

This was love and worship in action—an outpouring of devotion for the glory of God and the good of the world. Yes, we sang songs to Jesus, listened to teaching together, and came away with a very real hope that something powerful had happened *in* our lives at Passion. But we also left secure in the knowledge that something had happened *through* our lives. We knew that there were people and communities dotted all over the planet whose lives would be encouraged and enriched because of this simple communal giving.

As Louie announced the final totals, the whole room exploded with joy—not congratulating ourselves but simply rejoicing in what an incredible force the church can be *together*. It is the wisdom of God's kingdom economy in action. He was multiplying our little loaves and fishes as He always did, to feed those who are hungry and amaze those who are watching closely. The church became a mighty choir of kindness that day, our lives of compassion resounding far beyond the walls of the arena.

These are great moments for our faith—they give us a glimpse of the kind of thing Bill Hybels was talking about: The church can be a generous force to be reckoned with. The church can be a mighty river flowing through cities and nations with righteousness and justice left in its wake. We have many challenges and obstacles ahead of us both in our local communities and on a global scale. There are people being overlooked, abused, and rejected everywhere we look. Families are ripped apart by poverty and disease. Hearts are bound up by addictions that are slowly destroying them. There are natural disasters and moments of chaos breaking out all over this world. And faced with all of this, we could be tempted to think that these problems are just too big to tackle and too fearsome to engage.

But I believe that this is part of our divine purpose—the church of God has an awesome call to shine light in the darkest of places and bring hope and healing to the neediest of lives. Together we can rebuild places long devastated. The Spirit of the Lord God is upon us to bring good news, bind up broken hearts, and proclaim liberty for the captives. We can usher in beauty where there has only been ashes, and joy where there has only ever been despair. We can inject truth, compassion, and mercy into the bloodstream of our communities—and see the incomparable restoring power of Jesus at work through our lives. Standing in that arena at Passion that day, I saw a glimpse of this—and our eyes of faith opened once again to the possibilities of what could happen through a loving, united, healthy, and dynamic church.

Scripture is full of teaching about God's heart toward the poor and forgotten. The Word of God speaks so strongly on this issue in order to highlight just how much compassion God has for those who are defeated or downtrodden. Proverbs tells us:

> If a man shuts his ears to the cry of the poor,
> he too will cry out and not be answered.
> (Prov. 21:13)

And also:

> He who is kind to the poor lends to the LORD,
> and he will reward him for what he has done.
> (Prov. 19:17)

These are astounding statements. Who would think that God might close His ears toward the prayers of those who are not listening to the cries of the poor? And whoever heard of a person "lending" to God? Here is the self-sufficient King of all eternity who needs nothing from our human hands. It is an incredible concept, spoken strongly to drive the point home and make us listen. Both of these justice-centered proverbs are bold statements, making it very clear just how much God is with the needy.

When we engage with the poor and distressed, we become a window to the heart of God. We put on display His fatherly compassion and generous grace to a world of broken hearts and fallen lives. Our acts of kindness can't help but have an evangelistic dynamic to them, for every we time we touch a life, we communicate a God of compassion. And somewhere in the mix, we find worship also. For Jesus defines these gifts of mercy as acts of devotion:

"Whatever you did for one of the least of these
brothers [and sisters] of mine, you did for me."
(Matt. 25:40)

It is worship, evangelism, and justice all swirling together
in beautiful harmony. Our lives of justice can become not only
music to the ears of God, but also a soothing, healing symphony
played among the chaos of this world.

It is said that years ago a cynical journalist asked Mother
Teresa whether she was really doing much good in her works
among the destitute and dying in the slums of Calcutta, India. In
one way, this was a deeply offensive question to ask—for she and
her team had spent countless days and months and years of their
lives trying to give hope and dignity to the sick and dying of that
city. In another way it was perhaps a very realistic question—for
the job at hand was so huge and the resources seemed so small.
We can all develop the same negative outlook if we're not careful. We
can focus on the immense tasks at hand in this fallen world and
wonder if all our efforts are really ever going to enact the change
we long to see.

But Mother Teresa knew three things in that moment. First,
this work was her worship to God. With the words from Matthew's
gospel above obviously in mind, she once commented that each
person she nurses "is Jesus in disguise."[4] Secondly, she knew that
each person was unique and valuable in the eyes of God and that
even those she couldn't save from dying could have love and dignity
bestowed upon them. Perhaps the third thing that kept Mother
Teresa hopeful in the face of such a doubtful question was that she

saw the big picture. She was convinced that our individual lives offered up in love and service play an important part in the grand scheme of things. In her own words:

> We ourselves feel that what we are doing is just a drop in the ocean. But if that drop was not in the ocean, I think the ocean would be less because of that missing drop.[5]

Her humble and wise outlook in that moment is great news for us today. At times we may feel despondent that even our best efforts fall short, seeming like just a drop in the ocean. But the beautiful and inspiring truth is this: *The ocean is made up of many drops.*

5

WHO DO YOU SAY THAT I AM?

Most expectant parents spend a whole lot of time trying to figure out what to name the baby when he or she finally arrives. It's quite an art—because most people are looking for a great-sounding name that hasn't been underused or overused and a name that doesn't sound just plain silly.

Beth and I have five children (four sons and a daughter), so we've given over more time than most to this creative naming process. The first time around, it was the summer of the year 2000 and our baby girl was soon to arrive. We'd spent the previous nine months or so doing some serious naming research—but somehow came up with nothing. We'd listened to others for fresh names, read baby naming books, tried joining existing names together to form new ones, and even searched different languages and cultures to try to discover a lovely name for our little girl. But even though we'd had over 250 days to figure it out, we just couldn't find the name we wanted. Whenever I loved a name, Beth wouldn't find it appealing, and every time she developed a firm favorite, I could instantly find three or four reasons why there was "no way ever" we were going to name our daughter that!

You can imagine my frustration, as a person who loves to play around with words, when a day or two before the due date we still hadn't stumbled across the right name.

And then it happened.

As we sat waiting for the baby to arrive, I was reading a wallpaper brochure that happened to be lying there on the coffee table. This was not something I'd ever done before in my life (nor is it something I ever intend to do again). But right then and there it hit me. Staring me in the face was the name of a wallpaper pattern I immediately loved the sound of:

"Maisey."

Beth and I agreed it was a definite possibility, and we both really liked the sound of it. But what did it mean? Heading straight for the baby names directory, we discovered the meaning to be "pearl," and again, we both thought that was beautiful. Then came the clincher for me: The name spells the phrase "*Yes I am*" backward.

Now forgive me for thinking about wordplay when it came to the sacred occasion of naming our first child, but this was quite frankly irresistible. Even more brilliant was the fact that when later in life our daughter said, "*Yes, I am Maisey,*" the whole sentence would spell the same backward as it did forward. Our search was over! We had a lovely sounding name and, on top of everything else, some clever palindrome possibilities too. But most important of all, our daughter's name carried a lovely meaning.

The Names of God

The names of God are also packed with meaning. His titles are not just labels or words that He liked the sound of and chose at random. Each one is full of substance and meaning, pointing us to the very essence of who He is. God named Himself. And He meant every word.

He is Alpha and Omega, the First and Last, and the Ancient of Days. He is the Lord God Almighty, the One who was and is and is to come. He is Prince of Peace, Counselor, and Everlasting Father. He is Emmanuel, God with us. He is Jehovah Jireh, the Lord our Provider, and Jehovah Rophe, the Lord who Heals. He is Faithful and True, Father of Glory, Fountain of Living Waters. He is the God of all comfort, the God of our salvation, and God only wise. His names are like colors of the spectrum, each revealing a little more of why He is so completely worthy of our devotion.

In Psalm 9:10 the psalmist sings:

> Those who know your name will trust in you.

He does not mean that those who have memorized the names of God will somehow find their way to a place of faith and stability.

He is talking about those who *really know* the name of God—in other words, they know God's character, nature, and ways. When we come to trust and believe that our God is everything He says He is, our lives radically change. When we start to realize just how firm a foundation we live upon, that understanding gives us much faith and hope for the present and the future.

When we study a person for a while, we will likely find a chink in his or her armor—an inconsistency of some kind, sin, or an exaggerated claim. For although we each have admirable qualities, none of us are anywhere near as consistent as we would like to be. God, however, is different. Approached from any angle, our God is altogether glorious. Search for as long as you like, but you will find no gaps in His greatness and no limits to His love; no shady areas, no inconsistencies, and no missing the mark. He is perfectly constant in all of His ways. No fading. No faltering. No failing. No "off days." No shadow of turning. There has never been a lapse in His character nor a flaw in His seamless nature. He tells us He is holy, and that is the whole truth and nothing but the truth. He tells us He is love, and everywhere we look we will see that love. A. W. Tozer once put it like this: "God is never partly anything."

In a world where all others may falter or fail, Jesus remains constant. When we are inconsistent, still He remains utterly dependable and steadfast. Life is ever fragile and changeable, but He alone stands solid and secure. Our God is unshakeable, unchanging, unwavering, unfading, unfaltering, unswerving, and unending. He announces His faithfulness and is never found to be lacking. He is the spotless and unfailing King of glory. He is light, and in Him there is no darkness at all. He illuminates situations. He beautifies lives. He exposes and expels darkness. He brightens the path of those who seek Him. Wherever He radiates His glory, nothing stays the same. For now and all eternity, our God is everything He says He is.

This is good news for our world. Every day the newspapers reveal a fresh scandal: politicians' finances, a public figure caught in unfaithfulness. And each of us needs look no further than our own lives to find a person who is inconsistent. We are all something less than we hope or claim to be. Add to that all the uncertainties of culture around us—take for example the failing financial markets of recent years. It's a harsh and swift reminder that the things we so easily put our trust in can turn out to be untrustworthy. People can be flaky, and the fabric of our society is so fragile. But for all these uncertainties, standing strong right in the middle is our unfailing God—the One who holds all things together. Not only is He the opposite of our many inconsistencies, He is also the antidote and answer for them. When all around is sinking sand, He is our solid ground—the firmest foundation a life could ever be built upon. The writer of Psalm 62 affirms this very same truth:

> Find rest, O my soul, in God alone....
> He alone is my rock and my salvation;
>   he is my fortress, I will not be shaken. (Ps. 62:5–6)

In describing God as a rock and a fortress, the songwriter is creating an image of strength and security. His soul is very much at rest in this truth. And what result does this have in his life? How does this revelation affect the outlook of this worshipper? He declares with faith and confidence that "*I will not be shaken.*" The psalmist's trust in the strength of God creates a stable environment in which to live. He is not announcing that nothing bad will ever happen in his life. Instead, he is proclaiming that whatever situation may come his way, the power and might of his God will not be overwhelmed, and he himself will be on solid ground. The truth is this: The way we see God directly correlates to the way we approach each day. If we know His name is great and we lift our eyes to the big picture, we are likely to live with a sense of security in this life, resting on the unshakeable nature of Jesus. If, however, we don't truly know His name in the depths of our hearts and ultimately don't trust Him to be all that He claims to be, we will live a very different existence. Our lives will be darkened by clouds of fear, insecurity, and anxiety. The way we look at God deeply affects our whole perspective on life.

Holy Confidence

As the father of four energetic boys and a beautiful daughter, I am regularly jumped upon in the comfort of my own home. Often I will be minding my own business, perhaps walking past the stairs, when one of my sons will leap from a great height and land on me, trusting that I will catch him. Having gotten over the initial shock of being mugged in my own house by a person half my size, I've learned to take this activity as a huge compliment. It says so much about what they think of me and of what they consider me to be capable. Apparently, they even think I have eyes in the back of my head. When they launch themselves from the sixth or seventh step, they are counting on my strength and quick reaction to make sure they don't end up in a heap on the floor. I love their bounding confidence and enjoy the way it fuels a sense of carefree adventure in my children. I wonder if we could start to live the same way in God our Father. Could we be so convinced of His strength that we live with a new holy confidence? Could we become so utterly sure of Him that our lives are marked by some big, bold, and courageous leaps of faith?

Perhaps the *strength* of God is something we underestimate and underemphasize today. In Psalm 21, the worshipper cries out, "Be exalted, O LORD, in your strength" (Ps. 21:13). God's strength in the Old Testament is very clearly on display for all to see. We see Him bring victory on a battlefield and turn a weak army into a mighty winning force. But what does His strength mean in our own contexts today? What does it look like in your life or mine? I think that the strength of God manifests itself among us in at least three separate ways:

- It creates the possible
- It turns around the inevitable
- It overcomes the hostile

As Moses led the people of God out of the captivity in Egypt and to the edge of the Red Sea, there seemed to be no way through—but the strength of God held back the waters so that the

Israelites could cross over. In that moment the inevitable recapture they dreaded was flipped on its head, and they continued to live in their newfound freedom. And to cap it all off, when the Israelites were safely on the other side, God let the sea re-form, overcoming and overwhelming the Egyptians in their hostile pursuit of His people. This is the true strength of God in action, and we must apply these principles to our own lives. You may be at a complete loss as to how to go forward in a situation, but the strength of God can create a way. You may feel that in your current circumstance you will lose or that a certain person, stress, or pressure will gain a hold on you. But God in His mighty strength is able to maintain your freedom and turn around the seemingly inevitable. He can stand strong against the hostilities you may face in life, and He will overcome anything outside His plan for you.

We always talk of the love, peace, and grace of God at work in our lives and rightly so, for this is absolutely the case. But we would do well to take hold of His strength at work among us too and begin to live in a place of confident expectation.

A while back I cowrote a worship song called "Our God" with my good friends Jonas Myrin, Chris Tomlin, and Jesse Reeves. We started writing it in a hotel ballroom late one night after a conference session, and as we wrote, hotel staff hurried around everywhere getting ready for the next day's events. The song then sat in an unfinished state on my computer for the next seven or eight months, until one day we managed to complete it. I can remember now loving the strong declarations we made that night in the ballroom—and the truth that for God to be God He will inevitably be higher, greater, and stronger than all else around Him.

But when the bridge section of the song started to form, there was an even greater sense of excitement at the truths we sang:

> *And if our God is for us,*
> *Then who could ever stop us?*
> *And if our God is with us,*
> *Then what could stand against?*[1]

Often now when we lead this song, we see the same explosive reaction to these encouraging truths. The song seems to paint a picture of a powerful and glorious God and then helps us recognize just how much those amazing attributes count for something in our own lives. No one needs a small god. Small gods are blown over in the storms of life and hold out no hope for anyone. We need a big God—One who is strong and awesome in power. The good news is, this is exactly who we find in Jesus.

In the eighth chapter of Mark's gospel, Jesus asks His disciples many questions:

"How many loaves do you have?" (v. 5)

"Why does this generation ask for a miraculous sign?" (v. 12)

"Do you still not see or understand? Are your hearts hardened?" (v. 17)

"Who do people say I am?" (v. 27)

But the biggest question of all comes soon after, in the twenty-ninth verse:

"Who do *you* say I am?"

Jesus asks the very same question of you and me today. And this will become the greatest question that each one of us must answer. Our heart response to this will shape the entire course of our lives. Who do you say Jesus is, right here, right now? Is He strong and glorious enough to lead you through every valley and provide for you in every desert? Is He gracious and kind enough to be everything you need in every moment? Is He wise and powerful enough to devise perfect plans for your life and bring them all to fulfillment? Is He the Messiah, the long-awaited Savior that Peter recognized on that day?

The first step of worship is to affirm our faith in Jesus and acknowledge reverently that He is every single thing He ever claimed to be. The next step is to let our confidence in Him begin to infuse a hopeful, expectant confidence into our own walks of faith.

6

10,000 REASONS

My family and I live just outside the city of Brighton on the south coast of England. The area we live in is a pretty enough picture any day of the year, but every now and again it becomes a scene of absolute beauty.

A couple of months ago a deep, soft snowfall arrived during the night, and by morning, snow covered the entire village and surrounding hillsides in a blanket of pure, glistening white. Every single place we looked, the view was stunning. I'm no photographer, but that day I decided to venture out and try to capture on camera the beauty of the moment. I intended to take just a photo or two of some of the unspoiled snowy scenes close to our house, but it soon turned into a much longer episode as I wandered around from scene to scene, completely captivated by all that I laid my eyes upon. And I just couldn't stop taking pictures. I took close-ups of frozen spider-webs and intricate frost-covered branches, and I took wider shots of fields and hills. That morning presented some of the purest and prettiest landscapes I'd ever seen. And the small country lanes I was accustomed to walking down now looked like scenes straight out of the tales of Narnia. In the end I had to return home and get on with my work for the day—but I could have wandered around that village for hours on end, continually amazed by all that I saw.

The life of worship for Christians is very much the same. It is a life of wandering and wondering—journeying from scene to scene and taking time to explore the magnificence of God. With the eyes of our hearts fixed upon Jesus we will always be amazed by the things we see. *Literally always.* We will find His splendor, power, and love inexhaustibly captivating.

Archbishop William Temple once described worship as:

> the quickening of conscience by His holiness;
> the nourishment of mind with His truth;
> the purifying of imagination by His beauty;
> the opening of the heart to His love;
> the surrender of the will to His purpose—
> and all of this gathered up in adoration.[1]

William Temple's words here sum up so well the rhythm of revelation and response that we find in our worship of God. He names three ways we receive the revelation of God in worship: consciences quickened, minds nourished, and imaginations purified. And then he names three ways in which we bring a response to all that God reveals: opening our hearts, surrendering our wills, and engaging in the adoration permeating all. It's a rhythm found time and time again in the life of worship. We see, and we sing. We explore the ways of God, and we express our responses to Him. We wander out into the vastness of His glory, and we wonder how One so high and holy could involve Himself with the likes of us. Every step of the way we find another reason to declare His praise. We have never met One nearly as loving, and we have never encountered another remotely so glorious. In Jesus Christ we find majesty fusing with mercy, and kindness flowing with kingship. We see generosity streaming with humility, and grandeur infused with grace. Time after time we find ourselves making a joyful surrender of our hearts and offering up serious-minded adoration in His honor.

One of the qualities I most admire in a person, or indeed in a church congregation, is a *readiness* to worship. The writer of Psalm 65 declares that "praise awaits you, O God" (v. 1), and that is a fantastic posture of the heart for us to adopt when it comes to bringing devotion to the living God. In our worship of Him, ideally, we should not need warming up or any amount of coaxing. We should be there, ready and waiting, mindful of the many, many reasons there are to praise Him.

Several times at past worship events, I've met children whose bodies were wasting away to cancer but whose spirits lived entirely alive and free. Even at young ages, and in fragile states, these

children readily offered up thanksgiving and devotion to God. I felt
humbled that they asked to meet me, the "worship leader," when
that description more accurately fit them—for it was *their* example
that led *me* in worship. Similarly, I've led worship at memorial services for some of the most heartbreaking losses of loved ones—and
been amazed and inspired by the readiness of the family to offer
up devotion in such an intensely hard time. These people have
openly spoken of their confusion, heartbreak, and feelings of anger.
But from that place they stood ready to trust and adore God, the
One they knew did not diminish in power, love, or worth in that
moment. Healthy hearts of worship recognize that there will never
be a moment in all eternity when God is not worthy of praise. He
looks for a people who, even in the shadows of life, are ready and
able to offer up worship.

If I wake up one day and cannot think of a reason to bring
praise to God, then something is wrong with my spiritual outlook.
If we fumble around in the dark, struggling to find a reason to be
thankful, we can be entirely sure that the blockage lies at our end
of the pipeline. God's goodness and glory fly at us speedily and
steadily from every imaginable angle. Look deep into the truth of
Scripture, and you will find a reason for His praise on every single
page. Look up toward the wonders of nature, and you will see His
glory heralded by all the many masterpieces of His creation. Look
behind you at God's track record in your life, and you will see
His faithfulness woven like a thread through every single one of
your days. Celebrate the victories He won on your behalf. Look
straight ahead of yourself in faith, and you will see the future
shining bright with His promises. And remember what is in your

hands today, and you will see His daily provision at work in your life. Look into the faces of your loved ones and the ones who love you, and thank your heavenly Father who enriches your life. Look into the window of your own heart, and you will recognize His works on the inside of you ever since the day you surrendered to His holiness. See Him saving you, shaping you, teaching you, and leading you—without fault and without fail. Every single direction we look, we find another reason to exalt Him.

The writer of Psalm 103 exhorts us further on this journey:

> Praise the LORD, O my soul;
>> and all my inmost being, bless his holy name.
> Praise the LORD, O my soul,
>> and forget not all his benefits—
> who forgives all your sins
>> and heals all your diseases,
> who redeems your life from the pit
>> and crowns you with love and compassion,
> who satisfies your desires with good things
>> so that your youth is renewed like the eagle's. (vv. 1–5)

And the songwriter is only just getting started:

> The LORD works righteousness
>> and justice for all the oppressed....
> The LORD is compassionate and gracious,
>> slow to anger, abounding in love....

> He does not treat us as our sins deserve,
>   or repay us according to our iniquities. (vv. 6, 8, 10)

And we're still not done. Reasons for the praise of God continue to flow:

> The LORD has established his throne in heaven,
>   and his kingdom reigns over all. (v. 19)

The Psalms remind us that all the best worship songs recall the many reasons for His praise. I love writing worship songs. The runner Eric Liddell in the movie *Chariots of Fire* said, "When I run, I feel God's pleasure," and that's exactly the same sense I have when I am writing a song. I'm not sure that my job burns off quite as many calories, but I can spend five or six hours composing and mistakenly think only an hour or two has actually expired. I don't claim to be any kind of expert, but the fact remains that one of my favorite things to do in life is to find a way to speak to God, and speak about Him, in song. I find myself grasping for a heightened way to tell God I love Him. I long to wrap words around His wonders and string together sentences and melodies that will help me reach higher in my quest to worship Him through music. Language will always have its earthly limitations—but I love the challenge of molding it and stretching it to discover a fresh way of talking to God.

A great worship song paints a glorious picture of who He is—and then helps the worshipper respond to what he or she sees in that picture. I look at a song as a *chapel*—creating a space from which devotion can readily flow. But I am also aware that these songs can become *classrooms*—informing the mind and educating the heart about the many, many reasons for the worship of God. Writing worship songs will be a lifetime's quest, for there is always more to say and always a more heightened way to say it. Every time songwriters put down the pen, happy with a finished song of worship, there are a thousand more to write. We perspire and are inspired, as we keep returning to the creative challenge of declaring His worth with as much honor as we can muster.

King Solomon knew this same tension as he set out to build a magnificent temple for God in Old Testament times. We see his passion to construct a building that would point toward the glory of his God. He had in his heart a desire to create something epic:

> "The temple I am going to build will be great,
> because our God is greater than all other gods."
> (2 Chron. 2:5)

He wanted the temple to be an incomparable building— intricately designed down to the finest details and put together with the most elaborate and expensive of materials. Yet Solomon knew in his heart that even this would never match up to the majesty and splendor of his God. In the very next verse he confesses:

> "But who is able to build a temple for him, since the
> heavens, even the highest heavens, cannot contain
> him?" (2 Chron. 2:6)

Solomon aimed high, but in reality he knew he would never actually hit the mark. This is a healthy tension for all Christians to live in. In fact, there's not a pastor, poet, musician, or artist in the church who shouldn't be creating from this place inside. The eyes of our hearts must be open wide to the sheer majesty of the One we attempt to describe. But deep down we must face the weighty and wonderful reality that we will never quite get where we want to be. Every song, as grand as we may think it sounds at the time, is just the tiniest whispered echo when compared to the thunderous glory of the One we approach in worship. It is this challenge that keeps me going. I have written a couple of hundred songs in my life, but there is so much more to do. For I have recognized the glory of Jesus, and therefore in both quality and quantity I am nowhere near where I hoped to be. I am not ungrateful for the songs that have come along so far, but I have an insatiable desire to see if I can get just a little bit nearer to conveying the epic wonders of our God. Staying silent or sitting dormant is simply not an option. I love it when I meet worship songwriters the world over who have this very same passion in their hearts and wake up every day to this very same challenge. We must spur one another on to higher and greater music about our God.

Every time I write a worship song I feel as if I am out in those snow-covered fields, desperate to capture the wonders I encounter. "Just one more picture ... oh actually ... just one more ... but look at that scene over there ... just one more picture." And so on. My ambition is to continue framing the many glories of God in song, the very best way I can. For I know there will always be more to see, and therefore there will always be more reasons to sing about Him. If you have this quest in your own heart, in whatever medium it might be, and others around you affirm such a call on your life, I encourage you to give it everything you have.

Together let's take seriously the challenge to fill our local churches with big, biblical, poetic, passionate, and relevant worship songs. To fill our local churches with poems, stories, films, paintings, designs, sculptures, and sermons. Every moment of every day, more incentives to sing out His praise swirl all around us—*ten thousand reasons for our hearts to find.*

7

THE RULE OF FIRST THINGS

If you meet a Christian whose story is dull, reserved, and devoid of action, then there's something seriously wrong. God designed us to be fascinated with life, never bored with it. We are called to take great delight in looking outwardly and not simply living inwardly. We are to be characterized by hope and joy, not dragged down by cynicism and apathy. The kingdom life should flow with surprises and mark us with freedom and adventure.

Some look to Christianity and point to what they see as a restrictive lifestyle. And it's true; there are boundaries for the disciples of Jesus Christ. The road Jesus calls us to walk upon is a narrow one.

And yet there is also a wonderful paradox—for the life of holiness is not defined by limitations. We become free to run in the wide-open spaces of God. As *The Message* phrases it:

> We find ourselves standing where we always hoped
> we might stand—out in the wide open spaces of
> God's grace and glory, standing tall and shouting our
> praise. (Rom. 5:2 MSG)

While many who live without faith claim to live in freedom, look beneath the surface of their lives and you may find a different story. Some who at first seem to be having the time of their lives are in fact becoming slaves to habits or addictions, which eventually shrink their existences. Before long, a great price has been paid—as if they have sacrificed their future fulfillment on the altar of short-term thrill seeking. Jesus, of course, can restore anyone and redeem any situation. But the point here is this: Whether it be addictions, appetites, or other destructive sins, everyone has a master. We are all worshippers of something or someone, subjecting ourselves to whoever or whatever we bow our lives before.

Anything in our lives that we don't submit to the rule and reign of Jesus may in time become our master. Instead of permitting freedom, it may in fact take control of our lives and make us serve its bidding. If you have your heart set on something that takes your heart away from God, that *something* is an idol. At times, these are obvious things, though at other times they can be much more subtle. It could be a relationship that we know to be less than what God wants for us, or less than He requires from us. It could be a career plan that is the one thing you would never surrender if asked to by Jesus. It could be your bank balance or a destructive habit. If exalted to the place in your life where only God should be, none of these things will ever become a road to joy and fulfillment. Instead they are the passageways to shattered dreams and small, entrapped lives where thirsts are never satisfied and freedom is only ever superficially tasted.

As the great writer and thinker C. S. Lewis expressed it, "Idols [break] the hearts of their worshippers."[1]

Jesus, on the other hand, brings fulfillment to the hearts of His worshippers. Those who seek Him with all their hearts will find Him, and with Him they will find a future full of purpose and promise. C. S. Lewis also wrote this: "Put first things first and we get second things thrown in. Put second things first and we lose both first and second things."[2]

He was simply echoing the words of Jesus when He declared:

> "Seek first his kingdom and his righteousness, and
> all these things will be given to you." (Matt. 6:33)

In other words, if we will truly put God first and prioritize what He prioritizes, all the rest will take care of itself. See the story of King Solomon, for example. He used his one request to ask God for wisdom to lead the people of Israel. And because he prioritized God's priority, he received wisdom and so much more. His life overflowed with all kinds of abundance. This is an important truth we see echoed many times throughout Scripture. In fact, it's hard to overstate how important this truth is for us to get hold of. It is *the rule of first things.*

Second Things

So many times we are prone to choose other things—*second things*—and promise that once we have our grasp on these, then we will give our attentions to God. But it does not work like this, as God will not share His glory with another. And He will not be our second choice or backup plan. If we place Him first, we will see His pleasure in that choice overflowing into our lives.

At other times, we are prone to give up the fight and settle for something far less glorious and satisfying than what He offers us. Too many times I have seen people fail to receive the *second thing* they asked of God, and so they decided in response to give up on Him as the *first thing* in their lives. Perhaps they could not find a Christian spouse and so—out of desperation, or anger at God, or both—decided to settle for someone walking in the opposite direction. A choice from such a place seldom leads anywhere good.

Psalms 37 tell us:

> Delight yourself in the LORD
>   and he will give you the desires of your heart. (v. 4)

Perhaps there are two reasons this is the case. For starters, we have honored God by putting Him first, and in response He is happy to entrust us with these second things. But in addition, if we confess

Jesus as Lord and Master, all our other dreams and aspirations are unlikely to be at odds with what He stands for. Nor are they likely to be in competition with Him.

My Experience

Everything substantial that ever happened in my life took place as I put first the kingdom of God and tried to prioritize His kingdom and His righteousness over all else. I looked upon Him, and the rest took care of itself. I found an amazing wife, though at the time I wasn't really searching. I'd decided to become a full-time worship leader at my local congregation and help plant a church. I didn't have the time, money, or energy for much else, and strangely I wasn't worried in the slightest about that fact. I tried to fix my eyes on Jesus and figure out how to shape my life around serving Him and His church. And then suddenly, there she was—Beth Vickers, a beautiful worshipper of Christ whom I fell in love with and married. I looked up across the church parking lot one day, and walking toward me was this young lady who very quickly became a desire of my heart!

In the same way, when it came to a career path, I didn't have a big five-year plan up my sleeve. I simply focused on using my skills and my life to build the kingdom of God—and somehow a kind of job that I never really knew existed unfolded before my eyes. Leading worship and writing songs of devotion turned out to be the most fulfilling thing I could ever imagine, so much so that I couldn't believe they paid me to do it. In the beginning I covered some living expenses by doing this job, whereas today I have an income with which I can support my wife and five kids. I didn't go looking for how to grab a bigger paycheck. Nor was I trying to carve out some kind of purpose or role for myself. By the grace of God I tried to put first things first, and He took care of the rest.

I hope I don't sound simplistic or overly naive. But my little point is this: All I did was put my hand to the plow, prioritize my life around Christ and advancing His kingdom—*and the rest took care of itself.* I put my head down, served Him the best I knew how, and one day I looked up and realized that somewhere along the way, He'd graciously given me the desires of my heart. I am not at all trying to commend myself here—anything that turned out good in my life was wholly the grace of God at work. Instead I'm testifying to the true and effective words of Jesus. If we will seek Him and give Him the place at the head of our lives, He will provide everything we need and so many of the things we desire along the way. The kingdom of God is an abundant place to live. I don't know the exact route God has for your own life, and I'm not saying that choosing to walk this path is a guaranteed way to find a spouse or a certain kind of job. There may be times of waiting or confusion. There may be situations in which we don't get quite the thing we asked for and cannot understand it. But I do know that choosing Jesus as the first and foremost factor in your life will lead to a fulfilled existence and a tremendous amount of blessing poured out along the way.

And yet there is a paradox here too. For alongside all the blessing, choosing to prioritize Christ will also mean some scars and struggles on the way. Christians are not exempt from hardship—in fact, we are guaranteed it. Beth and I have had the privilege of helping start up several local churches, and we've also had the excitement of traveling to around thirty different countries as we've sought to respond to the call of Jesus. From the outside this looks like a dreamy life, and I won't deny there's been lots of fun and never a dull moment. But just as it has led to much joy and adventure, at times it has also involved much pain and cost. In several seasons the strain on our family from all this travel and transition and a few other obstacles along the way has been immense. I'm not in any way trying to stir up sympathy, nor am I wishing to paint a picture that we are something we're not. But I do want to give you the whole story.

Yes, Jesus promises His rest, His provision, and many a blessing for those who seek first His kingdom and righteousness. But we're also guaranteed some pressure along the way. As theologian Graham Tomlin notes, the more intensely we follow Jesus the more joy and laughter there will be, but likely the more tears and struggle also. Carrying His name in this world is an awesome and enjoyable adventure, but one that will require much endurance and courage.[3]

For some worshippers, the decision to place Christ over and above all has even led to martyrdom. Your own path of worship may not be as severe as that, but you can bet it will not always be a convenient journey. At the same time, for every single step along the way, you can count on the abundance and provision of God to be everything you'll ever need. He is a generous Father—whose eyes will always be upon us and whose kindness, power, and wisdom will always reign over us. His joy will be a breath of fresh air on our bright sunny days and strength for the journey on our cold winter nights. His goodness will follow us all the days of our lives, and His grace will always be enough. Anyone who ever invested his or her life in His kingdom and gave it all for His praise found one thing to be sure: You can never outgive God. Putting Him first may not always be the easiest decision, and it may not end up looking exactly how we envisaged. But it will never end in regret.

There's an encouraging and empowering motto the psalmist held on to that we would do well to etch upon our hearts today:

The LORD will fulfill His purpose for me. (Ps. 138:8)

The first step is to believe that He has a purpose written for your life. The second step is to trust and obey Him to bring that purpose to fulfillment.

Eternity with Jesus is, of course, the biggest prize, and the greatest wide-open space of all. But here and now upon the earth, worshipping Jesus Christ wholeheartedly will lead you through many adventures to many blessings and into a life of true satisfaction and fulfillment.

The road may be narrow—but *the possibilities are endless.*

8

ENDLESS HALLELUJAH

Ephesians 1 invites us into an epic drama, with many grand themes on display. We hear about creation, redemption, resurrection, adoption, and blessings in the heavenly realms. We discover a gospel of immense proportions and eternal possibilities. But astoundingly, these themes and activities are not simply happening in another sphere somewhere, nor are we just spectators getting a glimpse of the action. No! We are caught up right in the middle of it today. You have been adopted, redeemed, forgiven, lavished upon, and raised up with Christ.

We live our lives in both the *everyday* and the *eternal*. The *everyday* things are obvious. We wash, we eat, we work, we sleep, we talk, we move. We go about our daily activities, and the *here and now* is plain for us to see.

And yet we must also lift up our eyes and acknowledge the *eternal*. We are caught up in the glorious and unending big picture of the kingdom of God at work. We are never detached from this great reality. We are walking it, breathing it, living it. It is *not* more real in certain environments than in others. It is always true whether you spend your days studying for exams, looking after your kids, or recuperating in a hospital bed. You are caught up in this immense kingdom drama just as much when you wash the dog or crunch numbers at work as you are on a Sunday morning, singing songs in church that directly address these themes. Those Sunday moments are so helpful—for they remind us of the bigger picture.

As a songwriter one of my big quests is to write songs that *address the everyday but announce the eternal*. But we must grasp this seemingly paradoxical truth far beyond our church-gathering moments. Sometimes we move from one task to another and forget that for all our efforts at home, work, or college, a far greater narrative ties everything together. We must learn to see beyond mere physical realities and grasp the spiritual actualities of our lives. God, in His all-wise and all-loving ways, orchestrated a masterful and merciful gospel plan that is playing out even now—and amazingly you and I are caught up in it.

We are moving in the kingdom of God. His kingdom never retreats or goes stagnant for a moment—*it is always advancing*. And as we live, breathe, and work we are advancing with this kingdom.

First of all we need to gain a great big picture of God before us. But next we must come to grips with just how active and extensive His glorious kingdom is. Eugene Peterson writes: "If we calculate the nature of the world by what we can manage or explain, we end up living in a very small world."[1]

There is more going on around us than we could ever realize. God is at work. He is not distant, dormant, or docile. He never sleeps and never grows tired or weary. He is the powerful, promise-keeping, and change-breathing God. The doors He opens no one can close, and the doors He closes cannot be opened. His words never return to Him empty. He is always at work in you and all around you. The One who wove together the intricacies of this universe gets up close and personal and cares about the details of your situation. He is powerful and present; He is interested and involved. We must not exist merely on a diet of what we see reported on TV, what Internet blogs say, or what local conversations tell us. We must look up and see His bigger picture. As Peterson so eloquently expresses in another one of his books:

> [The kingdom] requires a total renovation of our
> imagination so that we are able to see what our eyes
> do not see, so that we are capable of participating
> in what will not be reported in tomorrow morning's
> newspaper.[2]

A Picture of Revelation

Perhaps nothing paints this grand, mysterious picture for us better than the book of Revelation in the Bible. At first glance this final book of Scripture can all seem a bit too much. Some of the episodes in Revelation are completely off-the-chart strange and mysterious. We are shown an incredible throne room with a multitude of colors, sights, and sounds swirling all around. We encounter creatures that are quite literally out of this world, creatures we are not accustomed to seeing—*especially not in Scripture*. There are strange fires, mighty earthquakes, and epic battles. We read about fearsome plagues and judgments. There are lively songs of victory and loud shouts of woe. And then we see a radiant holy city and a God who declares, "I am making everything new." It is a drama of enormous proportions. But we must not be daunted or intimidated by the awe-inspiring sights of this book. For one thing, Revelation reminds us of how the endgame plays out. We are not hanging in the balance until the final chapter of history unfolds, waiting and hoping that the result goes our way. The book of Revelation tells us of a victorious God who will carry out His purposes and win the day.

Nations may quake, economies may fail, marriages might split apart, and loved ones will slip away. Indeed, at the worst times in your life, your whole world might seem as though it is breaking and shaking apart. In such a time we need the calm, soothing oil of compassion poured over our hearts. But we also need the unbending and unbreakable truth of a God who is always in control. We may at times search through our Bibles for "comfort" verses in our troubled moments, and there's nothing wrong with that. But we must also turn in those unstable times to epic moments of Scripture like Revelation where we encounter this awesome God who reigns over all creatures. When everything else seems to be spiraling out of our control, He is just as strong, sure, and steadfast as He ever was. Before long our hearts take encouragement from the fact that this God who was and is and is to come is also the God of our yesterdays, the God of us here today, and the God of all our tomorrows. The God of forever is right here with us, right now. When we begin to see the unseen, we will live a whole different way. With this perspective, there comes a new sense of stability and constancy, which finds its way into every area of our lives.

We serve an everlasting King who cannot be taken by surprise. He is the Holy One who will never be outwitted, outmaneuvered, or overpowered. He is the victorious One, the high and mighty Creator who holds all things together. We find love that will not let us go, strength that will not let us fall, glory that will never fade, and hope that can never be stolen away. We see a Lamb who takes away the sin of the world, and a Lion mighty enough to rule over all things.

At times, our circumstances in life may cloud our view of this bigger picture.

My oldest son, Noah, has always been a bit of an early starter in the mornings. When at the age of four he started getting up a little too early for our tastes, we tried our best to convey to him that just because the sun had risen at 5:00 a.m., that didn't necessarily mean he needed to get up at the same time. At that age he couldn't tell the time on a clock, but I found what I thought to be a clever solution— a "bunny" alarm clock with ears that rose up at the set alarm time. So our simple instruction was that he could get up when the bunny's ears rose in the morning. However, I'd underestimated what a smart (and mischievous) little guy Noah was (and is).

A couple of mornings later, I heard him out of bed and playing loudly around the house at 5:00 a.m. yet again. As I entered his room, he confidently informed me that the bunny ears had risen and therefore he was allowed to do so. Taking a closer look, however, I soon realized that, despite the fact that he couldn't tell time, he'd figured out he could change the time and had skipped it forward a couple of hours. This way, when the alarm went off it was actually 5:00 a.m., not 7:00 a.m. But in all his childlike cleverness, he had underestimated one essential factor: *I have other time-keeping devices.* In fact one of these is an atomic-linked clock, which tells exact time down to the very second. So it didn't take me long to verify that the time was indeed 5:00 a.m. and that I would yet again have to devise a way to keep our little dawn raider in bed in the mornings.

The point of the story is simple: My brilliant son Noah could *mask* the true reality for a while, *but he could not actually change reality.* The very same thing is true with our lives. At times world events or our own life stories may seem as if they are spiraling out of control, and we can feel as if we are caught up in a series of random and confusing events with no purpose carrying us through. But a book like Revelation reminds us of a greater reality. It tells us that God is on His throne and very much in control of events. This is a truth that no one or nothing can ever change. God cannot be deposed, and His purposes cannot be derailed. He has won the victory, and everything else He means to accomplish will also come to pass.

We have been ushered into the big picture, and that is always a good thing for the heart of the worshipper. We must take the time to see that there is something far grander and more important going on around us than what our everyday activities will allow us to perceive. The book of Revelation unveils these spiritual realities and presents us with a holy and extraordinary God who has an unshakeable and unstoppable kingdom plan. His is the eternal kingdom that outlasts all temporary realities—a constant in the midst of our ever-changing circumstances. Amid the confusion of this fallen world, we see a refreshing picture of the rule and reign of our God on display.

Destiny in Our Daily Lives

We soon begin to see that our everyday moments can count for something eternally. We walk this earth with one eye on the horizon—aware of all that's going on around us in this world and in our individual situations—but knowing that God is working out His everlasting purposes. We will not become spiritual mystics unable to connect those heavenly scenes with our earthly existences—actually, quite the opposite. We will get a grip on the greatest reality of all, seeing *destiny* at work in the *daily,* and the *eternal* injected into the *everyday.* We will then walk in the knowledge that the sovereign One is unveiling His marvelous plans all around us and that even one act of compassion, one gospel-centered conversation, or one prayer of intercession could have eternal consequences in the life of someone we meet. In faith we start to believe that the salvation, hope, healing, and rescue of Jesus can break into the lives of our friends, families, or colleagues at any moment.

Never underestimate the kingdom of God at work. Many write off the worshipping bride of Christ, the church. They think the distinguishing marks of the church are scandal, numeric decline, and uninteresting or irrelevant teachings. In truth, there are decaying and diseased signs in some parts of the church, and it's a tragedy that those aspects are all some have seen of the body of Christ when they have glanced our way. But anyone who searches a little deeper knows there is a very different story to be told. There is a worshipping church that looks to Jesus and is being conformed to His likeness. The bride of Christ is radiant and beautiful even today. She speaks hope and truth to the lost and rejected. She binds up the wounds of the broken and remembers the forgotten. This church welcomes, worships, and works in powerful and life-changing ways.

We have a long ways to go, to be sure. I'm not blind to our weaknesses, and in no way do I want to diminish some of the awful abuses of leadership that have disillusioned so many and distracted from the gospel. We must deal with these things and never brush them under the carpet. But we must also look at the bigger picture and celebrate that we are, and are continually becoming, a radiant church. We are a city shining on a hill—reflecting the splendor and grace of the One we worship.

As C. S. Lewis put it: "We are mirrors whose brightness … is wholly derived from the sun that shines upon us."[3]

The church of God is not an age-old club that somehow manages to keep surviving through the ages. Instead, we are an ever-relevant and powerful force—right here and right now. And the radiance of Jesus continues to light up our little mirror-ball lives.

A Picture of the Nations

Growing up in the UK church, even amid a culture of secularism and cynicism, I have seen so much restoration and renewal. I've seen people healed, lives transformed, and communities enriched on so many different levels through the church. And over the years, I've had the privilege of traveling to more than thirty different nations to lead worship through music. It's interesting and inspiring to see so many different people and places—incredible oceans, cityscapes, and landscapes all over the world. But what has stayed with me most of all from these journeys is the beauty of the worshipping church. Touching down in so many different countries and cultures gave me a perspective of the big picture—and opened wide the eyes of my own faith. From Uganda to the Ukraine, the church is alive and well—being renewed and restored—and she is making a vital difference all around the world.

Of course, I've seen only the tiniest glimpse of the full reality—but in every single nation and city to which I've ever had the privilege of traveling, I've seen different expressions of that radiance. Seoul, South Korea, taught me some lessons in intercession—loud shouts of prayer accompanying loud lives of praise. Tokyo and Paris reminded me of how to shine brightly even in the most secular environments. The American church continues to lead the way in sending missionaries. And throughout the world, God has clearly broken the heart of His church for the poor and the forgotten—with so many worshippers seeking to become the hands and feet of Jesus to the least of these, the most disadvantaged among us. Everywhere I go, I see different emphases and different expressions of worship—but *one* worshipping church, serving powerfully and shining the heart of Jesus into the darkness. As we lift our eyes to the big picture, we realize just how much Jesus is at work building His church and advancing His kingdom around the globe.

Right here and now we sing our songs and realize that we are not just a group of believers singing alone or disconnected from the kingdom. We stand with the worldwide church and the saints of the ages. As we tune our hearts to heaven's song, we join the expressions of reverence and victory sung by elders and angels alike.

We begin to get a sense of what we are caught up in—but it is as if we're merely listening through a wall and straining to hear the full glory of what is occurring next door. We hear in part, and we sing in part. *But one day all shall be revealed.* We will turn the page of this songbook and find that the melodies and harmonies of God's great anthem are far, far greater than we have ever imagined. We will hear the full reality of this great song—every tribe and tongue, countless angels, and all creatures great and small caught up together in one glorious symphony before the King of all Kings:

> Then I heard every creature in heaven and on earth
> and under the earth and on the sea, and all that is in
> them, singing:
>
> "To him who sits on the throne and to the Lamb
> be praise and honor and glory and power,
> for ever and ever!" (Rev. 5:13)

The first and last signs of the kingdom to come are *worship*. When the Holy Spirit illuminates a person's life and that person chooses to put his or her faith in Christ, worship is the first activity that occurs. The very act of confessing Christ as Lord is the first glorious step on a lifelong journey of devotion to Him. But worship is also the last sign of the kingdom—*for we are told that it will endure forever.*

Evangelism is a sign of the kingdom but a temporary necessity here upon the earth. Justice and acts of compassion are also great signs, but no one will be in need of them in heaven. The same is true of healing—in heaven, every tear will have been wiped away, and there will be no sick or suffering to pray for. We will be left with worship—an unending song of praise forever reverberating around the throne of God.

It is the *endless hallelujah*—the song of all eternity.

DISCUSSION GUIDE

This discussion guide was created for use in small groups, but it may also be useful for individuals reading through this book alone. This guide uses each chapter of *Mirror Ball* and many of Matt's songs—including some of the very newest songs from his album *10,000 Reasons*—as a launching pad into honest discussion of the ideas, challenges, and biblical themes raised. If you're going through this guide with a group, your spouse, or a friend, try to remain open, honest, and compassionate in your discussion, and if you feel comfortable, pray through each session before you begin.

We are the risen

Living alive in You

And our passion will not die,

No our passion will not die.

Nothing can stop us;

We'll be running

through the night

And our passion will not die,

No our passion will not die.

Matt Redman and Jonas Myrin, "We Are the Free."

God who keeps our

fires burning,

Burning through the

darkest night,

See the hope in our hearts,

The faith in our eyes.

You can move the

highest mountain;

You can keep our dreams alive.

You're the joy of our hearts,

And You're the fire in our eyes.

Matt Redman and Jonas Myrin, "Fires."

1

THE PASSION OF THE CHRISTIAN

Questions

With your group or on your own, recall the story about Louie Giglio's mirror ball that Matt tells us at the beginning of chapter 1. Before the lights came on, Matt felt that the mirror ball was undersized, too small and insignificant to make a difference in that giant arena in Nashville.

1. Have you ever felt that way in your Christian walk? Do you ever feel too insignificant to make a difference for God's kingdom? Why or why not? Share

about the areas you have felt *significant* or *insignificant* in the past.

2. In terms of worship, mission, and your Christian life, what would you do if God shined His light on you and you could reflect it all around the world? If His light was enough to make a difference in any place, in any way through you, what mission-focused dream would you carry out in the world?

3. What massive problems would you attempt to tackle?

4. In chapter 1 Matt talks about a man who was attacked by a shark. The man screamed from the depths of his being, so loudly that the shark swam away and the man survived. Do you agree that Christians should worship from that deep place inside? If worship isn't necessarily about volume or energy, what does that mean to you?

5. If our worship truly came from that desperate and powerful place inside us, what would that look like in our lives and in our church services?

Thoughts

In light of Louie's definition that passion is "the degree of difficulty you are willing to endure to achieve the goal," consider what Jesus accomplished on the cross. How passionate, then, was Jesus to do His Father's will at the cross and to act out of love for us? Thinking about this, read through Mark 14 alone, and then discuss both the passion of Jesus and the passion of the disciples in this chapter with your group.

Then take a moment as a group to pray, and ask God to release more endurance, more love, and more passion for Him in your life.

You, O Lord, have made a way,

The great divide You healed;

For when our hearts

were far away

Your love went further still.

Yes, Your love goes further still.

Matt Redman and Jonas Myrin,
"You Alone Can Rescue."

You came to search and rescue

In love the Father sent You

Broke through the

darkest night.

You came to seek and save us,

You came to liberate us.

Jesus, You heard our cry.

Jesus, You heard our cry.

Matt Redman, Jonas Myrin, and Jason
Ingram, "Where Would We Be."

2

LOVE WILL GIVE ITS ALL

Questions

At the beginning of chapter 2, Matt writes about his newborn baby son, Levi, and the long, difficult fight for Levi's life during the pregnancy and his first few weeks and months. Matt writes about how it is a delight to expend energy and fight for his son because he loves him; in fact it isn't a labor at all—the struggle and difficulty are worth it.

1. Can you relate to this feeling of hard work and struggle given out of a deep love? What relationships require that in your life?

2. Later in that section, Matt quotes the following Scripture verse:

    It burns like blazing fire,
       like a mighty flame.
    Many waters cannot quench love;
       rivers cannot wash it away. (Song 8:6–7)

    What does this passage tell you about true love? When you think of your love for God, is it similarly powerful? Are you willing to scale great heights out of love for Jesus?

3. What do you think of our culture's example of love when compared to Jesus' example of love for us?

We see love in its purest form in what Jesus did for us on the cross. Matt describes the complexity of what Jesus did on the cross and how we can see themes of justice, sacrifice, suffering, obedience, endurance, and hope in His actions.

4. Discuss with your group, or think about on your own, how you see each of these unique and complex themes in what Jesus did on Calvary.

Thoughts

After Jesus' resurrection, Jesus talks with Peter and asks him, "Do you truly love me?" Peter responds by saying, "Yes, Lord." Jesus replies, "Feed my sheep." Read the text of John 21:15–17 and think about or discuss the meaning of Jesus' reply.

Then take a moment to pray, and ask God to help you to love others through your actions with Christ's pure love.

Magnificent—
You alone are holy,
No one else as glorious as You.
Magnificent—
Jesus, You are worthy,
Who can shine as
brightly as You do?
Magnificent—
You're so magnificent.

Matt Redman and Jonas Myrin, "Magnificent."

We've walked through storms,
And we have walked
through sorrows.
Still You won't let them
Steal away tomorrow.
We are going to shine,
Now we are going
to shine for You.
We leave the old behind,
It will not define us no.
Yesterday is gone,
Now anything possible.

Matt Redman and Jonas Myrin, "O This God."

3

BIG GOD, BIG LIFE

Questions

To illustrate the idea of taking up the challenge to live a big life for God, Matt describes at the beginning of chapter 3 John F. Kennedy's charge to go to the moon. As Matt says, human endeavor can take us to the edge of wonder, but worship of the almighty God takes us deep into wonder and worship in a way that nothing else can. And if we live for a big God, we ought to live big, adventurous lives, reflecting His radiance.

1. If it's true that God's massive, overpowering radiance overshadows any dullness inside us, does that give you more confidence in your Christian walk? If so, what does that confidence make you feel as if you *can* do today?

2. Read Psalm 18:29–33 and reflect on the things Scripture says we can do with God's help. Discuss or write down a list of the other things God has helped you accomplish already, or things He can help you accomplish in the future.

Recall the story about the four-minute mile in chapter 3. Once Roger Bannister broke the four-minute mile, a barrier people believed was impossible to break, dozens of others broke the four-minute barrier in succession soon after. The previous record of 4 minutes, 1.3 seconds stood for nine years until Bannister's accomplishment.

3. With this story in mind, how important do you think our attitude and mental state are as we look to take on challenging tasks for the kingdom? Why?

4. Read Numbers 14:24 aloud with your group or to yourself. What does God say about Caleb's attitude and "spirit" in this verse? How greatly does Caleb's faithfulness affect what God allows him to accomplish? Why do you think this is so?

5. How can you be sure that your trust in God's great power, your attitude toward seemingly impossible

tasks, will help you accomplish all that He desires for you?

Thoughts

God does not like to be underestimated, Matt writes near the end of the chapter. This is because when we wholeheartedly trust God against all earthly logic, and we allow Him to work in big ways in our lives, He is glorified! Take a moment to think through your life. In a moment of silent reflection and prayer, process your day, your week—and think about how you can more accurately estimate God's massive, unquantifiable power working in your life tomorrow.

Take a moment to pray about this, asking God for the confidence to act on an impossible goal for His kingdom. Ask Him for the opportunity to give Him more glory through your life!

We will shine like stars
in the universe,
Holding out Your truth in
the darkest place;
We'll be living for Your glory,
Jesus we'll be living for Your glory.
We will burn so bright with
Your praise, O God,
And declare Your light to
this broken world;
We'll be living for Your glory,
Jesus we'll be living for Your glory.

Matt Redman, "Shine."

Yes our God is
All He says,
All He says He is.
Jesus, in Your name we
could change the world.
We stand in Your love,
In Your power,
All You say we are.
Jesus, in Your name we
could change the world

Matt Redman, Jonas Myrin, and Jason
Ingram, "We Could Change the World."

4

DROPS IN THE OCEAN

Questions

In this chapter, the discussion turns toward what impossible things we can accomplish *together* as the church, just as the many agencies of the US government came together to achieve Kennedy's challenge to get to the moon. Recall the Bill Hybels quote Matt cites from the book *Courageous Leadership:* "Still to this day the potential of the local church is almost more than I can grasp. No other organization on earth is like the church. Nothing even comes close."

1. If the great potential of the church is still largely untapped, what does that mean for the problems of the world? Do you think the church could be seen as being complacent?

2. If you could mobilize even a portion of the church, or even just your own church, to achieve three goals locally or nationally (or globally!), what would they be? Write them down or discuss them as a group. What would be the best use of the church's influence if we wielded it *together* for the kingdom of God?

Next we see an example of this in the "Do Something Now" giving campaigns of the students of the Passion college movement. Twenty-two thousand college students raised over $1.1 million to help various causes around the world.

3. Why is it important for this message to sink in to the broader church? How could you see that happening?

4. Discuss ways you could challenge others in your church or city to think through this message and add their "drop" to the ocean. What kind of local projects in your area would change lives as well as open the door for you to share the gospel with others? Or you may want to get involved further afield. If you're looking for somewhere to start, check

out A21 (http://www.thea21campaign.org) or Do
Something Now (http://www.268generation.com/
passion2010/dosomethingnow/).

Thoughts

In our culture today people are often very isolated and can see many
barriers to working with others. Pray about Matt's challenge to join
the broader church in taking up big dreams for the kingdom of God,
and ask God for opportunities to pool your talents and resources
with others. Together we can accomplish so much more than we can
by ourselves!

Who shall we say You are?

You're the Living God.

Who shall we say You are?

You're the Great I Am.

The highest name of all;

You're all You say You are.

Matt Redman, Jonas Myrin, and
Jason Ingram, "Holy."

And if our God is for us,

Then who could ever stop us?

And if our God is with us,

Then what could

stand against!

And if our God is for us,

Then who could ever stop us?

And if our God is with us,

Then what could

stand against!

Matt Redman, Jonas Myrin, Chris Tomlin,
and Jesse Reeves, "Our God."

5

WHO DO YOU SAY THAT I AM?

Questions

God is unchangeable, spotless, unfailing, and steadfast, and this is good news for our world today. We live in a world in which everyone falls short and the newspapers reveal scandals about politicians, rock stars, church leaders, and all kinds of public leaders every day. But we have to remember, as Matt writes, that "when all around is sinking sand, He is our solid ground."

1. How we see God is critical when life gets tough. If we see Him as great and act as though He is who He says He is, that perspective will shape everything about our lives. So how do you see God? What names do you use when you pray to Him? Why?

2. God is described as a strong tower in the Bible, and He declares that He "will never be shaken." How should this affect your daily life? Does this change how you face the storms of your life?

Midway through this chapter Matt describes how his sons surprise him in his own home by jumping on him from great heights. Their leaps from the top of the stairs imply that they trust their father to catch them, no matter what.

3. When you hear this analogy, what does it make you think about? Reflect on this story and what it says to you—and write down your thoughts and impressions—or discuss it aloud with your group.

4. If we're living with childlike faith and trust in God, what sorts of leaps is He encouraging us to take right now?

Thoughts

What sorts of practical steps can you take to infuse your life with a hopeful, expectant confidence? Say a thankful prayer to God every morning, or read the many grand names of God aloud each evening. Regularly read Scripture passages proclaiming His awesome power, or memorize verses that give you confidence so you can call on them when you need them.

Pray aloud with your group or on your own as you humbly ask God to instill a deep confidence in you, a confidence rooted in His strength.

You're rich in love,
And You're slow to anger;
Your name is great,
And Your heart is kind.
For all Your goodness
I will keep on singing
Ten thousand reasons
For my heart to find.

Matt Redman and Jonas Myrin, "10,000
Reasons (Bless the Lord)."

Standing on this mountain top,
Looking just how far
we've come,
Knowing that for every step
You were with us.
Kneeling on this battleground,
Seeing just how much
You've done,
Knowing every victory
Was Your power in us.

Matt Redman, Jason Ingram, and
Tim Wanstall, "Never Once."

6

10,000 REASONS

Questions

This is a chapter about worshipping God and the many things in this life and in the universe that drive us to that place of awe, wonder, and an overwhelming sense of God's glory. As Matt writes, "God's goodness and glory fly at us speedily and steadily from every imaginable angle."

1. What things lead you to worship God in the first place? And while you're singing songs about God's

glory, wherever that act might take place for you, what thoughts take you deeper into focusing completely on Him?

2. In the middle of your everyday routine, what is it that makes you suddenly—and perhaps even surprisingly—stop and praise God in amazement? Begin your own list of ten thousand reasons in a journal or diary. Add all your answers to the above questions to the list, and also add to the list as you go through your day and your week.

Midway through this chapter, Matt writes this line: "One of the qualities I most admire in a person, or indeed in a church congregation, is a *readiness* to worship."

3. What does that phrase—"a readiness to worship"— mean to you? Think about this line and how it could apply to more than just singing songs to God and about God. How can you cultivate a readiness to worship not only personally but also in your community and your church?

4. Matt describes how he feels called to write about God's greatness through song, even though he could never write enough songs to fully capture God's glory. What do you feel called to do to try to communicate, share, or understand God's greatness?

5. Reread 2 Chronicles 2:5–6 and ponder Solomon's questions in these verses. He writes that the temple he plans to build will not be able to contain God. But Solomon continues and says that the highest heavens themselves cannot contain Him! When you think about our God, the One who simply cannot be contained because of His greatness, how do you feel?

Thoughts

Now that we've discussed the uncountable reasons we have to worship God, praise Him with all you've got! Seek to cultivate that sense of readiness in your life. Can you worship anywhere and at any time? Then why not prepare yourself and be ready to worship throughout your day? Keep your journal handy and whenever it strikes you, continue to build your list of ten thousand reasons as a regular act of worship.

Now pray with your group, or pray on your own, and thank God for some of the many reasons you stand ready to worship Him today.

I'm coming back to the
heart of worship,
And it's all about You,
All about You, Jesus.
I'm sorry, Lord, for the
thing I've made it,
When it's all about You,
All about You, Jesus.

Matt Redman, "The Heart of Worship."

To You our hearts are open,
Nothing here is hidden.
You are our one desire.
You alone are holy,
Only You are worthy;
God, let Your fire fall down.

Matt Redman, Jesse Reeves, Tim Wanstall,
and Matt Maher, "Here for You."

7

THE RULE OF FIRST THINGS

Questions

Recall the discussion of the Rule of First Things in this chapter. Simply put, the rule is this: If we put God first and prioritize the things He prioritizes, everything else will take care of itself. As C. S. Lewis wrote: "Put first things first and we get second things thrown in. Put second things first and we lose both first and seconds things."

1. If you put God and His priorities first in your life, does that guarantee you a life free of hardship and

struggle? If we prioritize our lives this way, what guarantees should we expect?

2. Read Matthew 6:31–34 to yourself or aloud with your group and then discuss. Talk or think about verse 33 and what this means in light of what you read in chapter 7. What things in your life would you say are second things and how should you treat them?

Take a moment and reread Matt's description of his own life in the section called "My Experience" in chapter 7. In this section he describes the path his own life has taken whenever he's chosen to put God first and prioritize His priorities. He writes that "choosing to walk this narrow road leads to the wide-open spaces of God."

3. Do you trust that God will carry out His plan for you when you put Him first? Why or why not?

4. Read Psalm 138 and reflect on the promise that God "will fulfill his purpose for me" (v. 8). Do you believe that going about life in this way is naive or simplistic? Do you think God will honor your trust in Him?

Thoughts

Take some time to talk to God and thank Him for His awesome ways, which are so great that they are entirely unfathomable to us.

Thank Him for the plans that He has for your life and for the possibilities open to you on your journey with Jesus. Finally, tell Him how much you trust Him, how you will obey Him, and how you will follow His leading no matter what comes at you in this life.

When this passing
world is over,
We will see You face to face.
And forever we will worship;
Jesus, You are all to us.
Jesus, You are all to us.

Chris Tomlin, Matt Maher, Matt Redman,
and Jesse Reeves, "'All to Us."

When I stand before Your throne,
Dressed in glory not my own,
What a joy I'll sing of on that day;
No more tears or broken dreams,
Forgotten is the minor key,
Everything as it was meant to be.
And we will worship,
Worship,
Forever in Your presence
we will sing.
We will worship,
Worship You,
An endless hallelujah to the King.

Matt Redman, Jonas Myrin, Tim Wanstall,
and Chris Tomlin, "Endless Hallelujah."

8

ENDLESS HALLELUJAH

Questions

In chapter 8 Matt introduces the dual ideas of the *everyday* and the *eternal* and how the kingdom of God is at work in our daily lives. God's kingdom is advancing at all times and is at work as much when you're washing the dishes as when you're at church on Sunday morning. God is interested and involved in your life right now.

    1. How can we remember God's grand narrative, which ties all things together, and better see the

eternal in our everyday? Is there a way to remind yourself of this truth practically, every day?

2. Eugene Peterson says: "If we calculate the nature of the world by what we can manage or explain, we end up living in a very small world." Do you agree with this statement and what it implies? What could this implication mean for you today?

In the book of Revelation, we read about massive battles, strange creatures, fires, earthquakes, plagues, judgment, and incredible epic events featuring multitudes of people and angels and other beings singing great songs of praise to God. This book is unlike any other in the Bible; however, it reminds us of the eternal endgame of God's kingdom plan. It reminds us that God will carry out his plans and be victorious!

3. How can the bigger-picture perspective given by the book of Revelation help us as we navigate our everyday troubles? Why do you think it's important to remember this eternal perspective?

4. When things get difficult, we must remember that bigger things are going on all the time. Look back over your answers to the previous questions. Write a list of the things you want to attempt for God with this eternal perspective, together with your church, knowing He can do anything, and with a holy confidence that He is always with you and has a plan for your life.

Thoughts

Take a few moments as a group or on your own to reflect on the bigger picture of God's eternal kingdom plans as you look at the week before you. Then pray over your week with this perspective in mind. Finally, pray over your list of ideas, thoughts, prayers, and goals for your life as you close out your study time. Give this list to God and go forward with confidence in His plan for you.

NOTES

Chapter 1

1. Eugene Peterson, *Where Your Treasure Is* (Grand Rapids, MI: Eerdmans, 1993), 30.

Chapter 2

1. Charles Spurgeon, *The Power in Praising God* (New Kensington, PA: Whitaker House, 1998), 48.

Chapter 3

1. John F. Kennedy, "Special Message to Congress on Urgent National Needs," May 25, 1961, transcript, John F. Kennedy Presidential Library and Museum, http://www.jfklibrary.org/Research/Ready-Reference/JFK-Speeches/Special-Message-to-the-Congress-on-Urgent-National-Needs-May-25-1961.aspx.

2. George Whitefield, quoted in Arnold Dallimore, *George Whitefield* (Wheaton, IL: Crossway, 1990), 27.

3. John Richard Andrews, *George Whitefield* (New York: Elibron Classics, 2005), 395.

4. John Newton, quoted in Andrews, *George Whitefield*, 397.

5. Andrews, *George Whitefield*, 417.

Chapter 4

1. Christopher Riley, "The 400,000 Strong Backup Team," guardian.co.uk, July 2, 2009, http://www.guardian.co.uk/science/2009/jul/02/apollo-11-back-up-team.

2. Simon Schama, *The American Future: A History,* directed by Sam Hobkinson and Ricardo Pollack (UK: BBC Warner, 2009), DVD.

3. Bill Hybels, *Courageous Leadership* (Grand Rapids, MI: Zondervan, 2002), 23.

4. Gwen Costello, *Spiritual Gems from Mother Teresa* (New London, CT: Twenty-Third Publications, 2008), 28.

5. Mother Teresa, *A Gift for God* (New York: HarperCollins, 1996), 40.

Chapter 5

1. Matt Redman, Jonas Myrin, Chris Tomlin, Jesse Reeves, "Our God," *Passion: Awakening* © 2010 Sparrow Records/sixstepsrecords.

Chapter 6

1. William Temple, *Readings in St. John's Gospel,* 1st series (London: Macmillan), 68.

Chapter 7

1. C. S. Lewis, *The Weight of Glory* (New York: HarperCollins, 1976), 31.

2. C. S. Lewis, *Letters of C. S. Lewis* (New York: Harcourt, Brace & World, 1966), 228.

3. Reverend Dr. Graham Tomlin, dean of St. Mellitus, email message to author, March 2011.

Chapter 8

1. Eugene Peterson, *Practice Resurrection* (Grand Rapids, MI: Wm. B. Eerdmans, 2010), 54.

2. Eugene Peterson, *Tell It Slant* (Grand Rapids, MI: Wm. B. Eerdmans, 2008), 129.

3. C. S. Lewis, *The Four Loves* (New York: Harcourt, Brace, 1960), 131.

ABOUT THE AUTHOR

Matt Redman is married to Beth, and they have five children: Maisey, Noah, Rocco, Jackson, and Levi. Based in Brighton, England, they are part of St. Peter's, a new church planted out of Holy Trinity Brompton in London. They are excited about the challenge of working in a city that is currently one of the most unchurched in the UK. Previously they were part of Passion City Church in Atlanta, Georgia, with pastors Louie and Shelley Giglio, and they continue to work alongside the Passion movement.

Matt has been leading worship full-time since the age of twenty, and this journey has taken him to countries such as South Africa, Japan, India, Australia, Germany, Uganda, Croatia, and the Czech Republic.

His early compositions include songs such as "The Heart of Worship," "Better Is One Day," and "Once Again." More recent songs have included "Blessed Be Your Name" and "You Never Let Go"—both written with his wife, Beth, to encourage Christians to worship God through the storms of life. As Matt explains, "'Blessed Be Your Name' is a declaration of something that we've both found to be true in the tough seasons of life—that to worship God and trust Him no matter what is always the best path to take. The song

'You Never Let Go' takes up the same theme—it starts off with some thoughts from Psalm 23 and reminds us that no matter what we come across in life, there is a God who is in control, closer than we could ever know, and holding us." Most recently, Matt has written songs such as "You Alone Can Rescue" with regular cowriter Jonas Myrin and "Our God" with Myrin, Chris Tomlin, and Jesse Reeves.

Matt is also the author of several books, which all center around the theme of worship. *The Unquenchable Worshipper* unpacks what a healthy heart of worship might look like and how that translates into the lives we lead. *Facedown* explores how we can paint a big picture of God through both our songs and actions. The third book, *Blessed Be Your Name*, coauthored with Beth, is an encouragement to trust in the sovereignty and goodness of God, even when doing so seems costly. Matt has also compiled two other books—*The Heart of Worship Files* and *Inside-Out Worship*—both of which contain practical worship-leading advice from many experienced leaders from around the globe.

SONG BIBLIOGRAPHY

10,000 Reasons (Bless the Lord). Written by Matt Redman and Jonas Myrin © 2011 Thankyou Music (PRS) (admin. worldwide at EMICMGPublishing.com, excluding Europe, which is admin. by Kingswaysongs) / sixsteps Music / worshiptogether.com; Songs / Said And Done Music / Shout! Publishing (ASCAP) (Admin. at EMICMGPublishing.com).

All to Us. Written by Chris Tomlin, Matt Maher, Matt Redman, and Jesse Reeves © 2010 sixsteps Music / worshiptogether.com; Songs / Said And Done Music / Vamos Publishing (ASCAP) / Valley Of Songs Music (BMI) (Admin. at EMICMGPublishing.com) / Thankyou Music (PRS) (admin. worldwide at EMICMGPublishing.com, excluding Europe, which is admin. by Kingswaysongs).

Endless Hallelujah. Written by Matt Redman, Jonas Myrin, Tim Wanstall, and Chris Tomlin © 2011 Thankyou Music (PRS) (admin. worldwide at EMICMGPublishing.com, excluding Europe, which is admin. by Kingswaysongs) / sixsteps Music / worshiptogether.com; Songs / Said And Done Music / Shout! Publishing / Vamos Publishing (Admin. at EMICMGPublishing.com) / Chrysalis Music LTD (ASCAP).

Fires. Written by Matt Redman and Jonas Myrin © 2011 Thankyou Music (PRS) (admin. worldwide at EMICMGPublishing.com, excluding Europe, which is admin. by Kingswaysongs) / sixsteps Music / worshiptogether.com; Songs / Said And Done Music / Shout! Publishing (ASCAP) (Admin. at EMICMGPublishing.com).

Heart of Worship. Written by Matt Redman © 1999 Thankyou Music (PRS) (admin. worldwide at EMICMGPublishing.com, excluding Europe, which is admin. by Kingswaysongs).

We Are The Free. Written by Jonas Myrin and Matt Redman © 2011 Thankyou Music (PRS) (admin. worldwide at EMICMGPublishing.com, excluding Europe, which is admin. by Kingswaysongs) / sixsteps Music / worshiptogether.com; Songs / Said And Done Music / Shout! Publishing (ASCAP) (Admin. at EMICMGPublishing.com).

We Could Change the World. Written by Matt Redman, Jason Ingram, and Jonas Myrin © 2011 Thankyou Music (PRS) (admin. worldwide at EMICMGPublishing.com, excluding Europe, which is admin. by Kingswaysongs) / sixsteps Music / worshiptogether.com; Songs / Said And Done Music / Shout! Publishing (ASCAP) (Admin. at EMICMGPublishing.com) / Sony ATV Timber Pub (ASCAP).

Where Would We Be. Written by Matt Redman, Jason Ingram, and Jonas Myrin © 2011 Thankyou Music (PRS) (admin. worldwide at EMICMGPublishing.com, excluding Europe, which is admin. by Kingswaysongs) / sixsteps Music / worshiptogether.com; Songs / Said And Done Music / Shout! Publishing (ASCAP) (Admin. at EMICMGPublishing.com) / Sony ATV Timber Pub (ASCAP).

You Alone Can Rescue. Written by Matt Redman and Jonas Myrin © 2009 Thankyou Music (PRS) (admin. worldwide at EMICMGPublishing.com, excluding Europe, which is admin. by Kingswaysongs) / sixsteps Music / worshiptogether.com; Songs / Said And Done Music / Shout! Publishing (ASCAP) (Admin. at EMICMGPublishing.com).

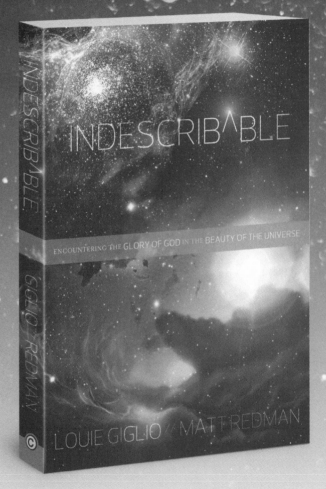

DO SOMETHING
NOW

Do Something Now is a movement rooted in the belief that together we are a force for good! To introduce ourselves, we are the Passion Movement, and to many we are known for worship. That having been said, our desire is to make sure that if we are going to be known as a worship movement,

THE WORSHIP WE WANT TO BE KNOWN FOR IS WORSHIP THAT WEDS SONGS WITH ACTION.

We love music, and have been privileged to bring many new songs to people around the globe. But we are convinced that worship is about more than music, worship is love in motion. It's clear that the kind of worship God wants most requires more than words, calling us to love the world in Jesus' name. The desire of Do Something Now is to open the door as wide as we can, inviting everyone to join in the movement. You don't have to be university-aged or attend one of our events to impact those in need. You're here, and you can join the movement wherever you are. This is hope of a brand new life for people who cannot help themselves. None of us can do it alone. Follow your heart. Do Something Now.

dosomethingnow.com

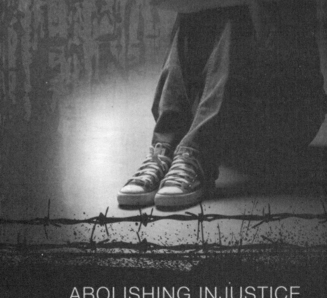

99% OF **TRAFFICKED VICTIMS** ARE **NOT** RESCUED...**YET**

ABOLISHING INJUSTICE
IN THE 21ST CENTURY

WWW.THE**A21**CAMPAIGN.ORG